FRAUD!

FRAUD!

HOW TO PROTECT YOURSELF FROM SCHEMES, SCAMS, AND SWINDLES

MARSHA BERTRAND

AMACOM

American Management Association

New York • Atlanta • Boston • Chicago • Kansas City • San Francisco • Washington, D.C.

Brussels • Mexico City • Tokyo • Toronto

Special discounts on bulk quantities of AMACOM
books are available to corporations, professional
associations, and other organizations. For details,
contact Special Sales Department, AMACOM, an
imprint of AMA Publications, a division of
American Management Association,
1601 Broadway, New York, NY 10019.
Tel.: 212-903-8316   Fax: 212-903-8083

This publication is designed to provide accurate and authoritative
information in regard to the subject matter covered. It is sold with the
understanding that the publisher is not engaged in rendering legal,
accounting, or other professional service. If legal advice or other
expert assistance is required, the services of a competent professional
person should be sought.

Library of Congress Cataloging-in-Publication Data

Bertrand, Marsha.
    Fraud! : how to protect yourself from schemes, scams, and
swindles / Marsha Bertrand.
        p.   cm.
    Includes index
    ISBN 0-8144-7032-7
    1. Fraud. 2. Fraud—Prvention. 3. Swindlers and swindling. .
4. Commercial crime. 5. White collar crime. I. Title.
HV6691.B47 1999
16'3—dc21   99-34601
                                                                CIP

Printing number

10 9 8 7 6 5 4 3 2 1

DEC 0 2 1999

CONTENTS

PREFACE

Right or wrong, a good persuader is still a good persuader.

ROBERT HALF, JOB PLACEMENT AUTHORITY AND AUTHOR

Whether we like it or not, money is an important part of our lives. Without it we can't obtain shelter, food, clothing, or transportation. Our very lives depend on it. But money can be difficult to come by; it takes hard work and long hours. When we're stripped of our money by fraudulent means, the consequences can be devastating. In fact, economic crimes can be just as emotionally devastating as violent crimes. A family that has saved for years to buy a house, send a child to college, or create a comfortable retirement may suddenly see those plans disappear because they were trusting and made one bad decision.

Our odds of becoming the victim of an economic crime are much greater than becoming the victim of a violent crime. A mugger can mug only one person at a time, but a con artist can defraud hundreds of people out of their money at once. And because victims are often unwilling to come forward and admit they were scammed, many con artists remain free to continue victimizing people.

The truth, however, is that even if all frauds were reported, the majority of the perpetrators would go free because the authorities empowered with prosecuting these people have far too few resources and personnel to handle all the economic crime that exists. That means we all have to be responsible for protecting ourselves from these con artists. We need to educate ourselves and know what to look for. If more people learned how to identify and avoid a scam, the number of potential victims would dwindle. And without victims, con artists are out of business.

Part One of this book discusses what fraud is, how much exists, and who perpetrates it. Parts Two through Six look at some targeted victims and examine the various types of frauds that are prevalent in the marketplace today: affinity fraud, Ponzi and pyramid schemes, commodity fraud, high-tech fraud, and more. You'll find that many of these frauds are interconnected. Affinity fraud can be a Ponzi scheme, elder fraud can be micro-cap stock fraud, and high-tech fraud can be a business opportunity fraud. Part Seven discusses the tools con artists use to perpetrate their frauds, and Part Eight tells us how we can protect ourselves from fraud and, what to do and whom to turn to if we find we've been defrauded. Finally, Part Nine tells us how to find and work with a trustworthy stockbroker and financial planner, and suggests future types of fraud we may need to be aware of.

Although some of the names have been changed throughout the book to protect certain identities, the stories are all true. And just like you and me, the victims in these stories never thought they could ever be swindled or scammed. But at some point, the con artist came knocking on their doors.

Are those footsteps I hear coming up your front walk? Quick! Read on!

ACKNOWLEDGMENTS

When bad men combine, the good must associate,
else they will fall one by one,
an unpitied sacrifice in a contemptible struggle.

EDMUND BURKE, CONGRESSMAN

My thanks to all the experts who took the time to be interviewed, share their expertise, read manuscripts, and lead me in the right direction. These people work hard every day to fight fraud and help those who become victims. Thanks to the victims of fraud who were courageous enough to share their stories. And thanks to the con artists who were willing to admit their pasts and give us an insight into fraud from their point of view. I appreciate everyone's willingness to help this book become a reality:

Alexandra Armstrong, certified financial planner, Armstrong, Welch, and MacIntyre; columnist and author

Marc Beauchamp, communications director, North American Securities Administrators Association

Jules Burstein, clinical and forensic psychologist

Brett Champion, president, Champion Entertainment

Brent Collier, chief of police, Milwaukee, Oregon

Larry E. Cook, director of the Enforcement Division of the

Office of the Kansas Securities Commissioner

Don DeBolt, president, International Franchise Association

Courtney Ford, Certified Financial Planner Board of Standards

Beth Givens, executive director, Privacy Rights Clearinghouse

Bob Goss, president, Certified Financial Planner Board of Standards

Susan Grant, director, National Fraud Information Center and Internet Fraud Watch Programs, National Consumer League

David Grauer, enforcement director, Texas State Securities Board

Timothy J. Healy, supervisory special agent and program manager for telemarketing fraud, Federal Bureau of Investigation

Leatha Hein, trustee of Mid America Yearly Meeting of Friends, Valley Center, Kansas

Dick Johnston, director, National White Collar Crime Center

Bronti Kelly, Temecula, California

Jane Kusic, founder and president, White Collar Crime 101

Dan Langan, director of public information, National Charities Information Bureau

Barry Minkow, senior pastor, Community Bible Church, San Diego

Janet Mortenson, attorney, Houston, Texas

Barbara Morton, vice president of housing and education, Consumer Credit Counseling Service of Central Florida

John Moscow, assistant district attorney, New York County District Attorney's Office

Jay Oman, assistant director of enforcement, Texas State Securities Board

Balde Quintanilla, investigator, Enforcement Division, Texas State Securities Board

Jonathan Saffold Sr., pastor, Ebenezer Church of God in Christ, Milwaukee, Wisconsin

Mary L. Schapiro, president, National Association of Securities Dealers (NASD) Regulation, Washington, D.C.

Steven Toporoff, franchise program coordinator, Federal Trade Commission, Bureau of Consumer Protection

Michelle Walensky, Fugitive Publicity Unit, FBI Headquarters

Joseph T. Wells, chairman and founder, Association of Certified Fraud Examiners

Chuck Whitlock, investigative reporter, *Extra*

Paul N. Young, founder and CEO, Securities Arbitration Group and National Mediators Group

Special thanks go to the following five experts who generously took time from their busy schedules to answer my constant questions, read manuscripts, and offer any assistance I requested:

Philip A. Feigin, executive director, North American Securities Administrators Association, and former Colorado securities commissioner

Ronald V. Hirst, associate general counsel and enforcement coordinator, National Futures Association

Andrew Kandel, chief of the Investor Protection and Securities Bureau, New York State Attorney General's Office

Ralph Lambiase, securities director, Department of Banking, State of Connecticut

Bill McDonald, enforcement director for the California Department of Corporations (the state securities regulator for California)

My biggest thanks goes to Denise Voigt Crawford, Texas state securities commissioner and president of North American Securities Administrators Association, who agreed that this project was important and offered to devote her time and expertise to it. Without her help, this book might never have been written.

Thanks to Ray O'Connell at AMACOM, who liked the idea and convinced his colleagues it was a viable and worthwhile project.

Thanks to my agents and friends, Nicholas Smith and Andrea Pedolsky of Altair Literary Agency in New York. I appreciate their guidance and belief in my work.

And finally, thanks to my husband, Gary, who put up with months of having to deal with a wife with a one-track mind. I sincerely appreciate his patience, support, and encouragement.

PART ONE

IT ALWAYS HAPPENS TO THE OTHER GUY

CHAPTER 1

The Business of Fraud

*The power of accurate observation is commonly called
cynicism by those who have not got it.*

GEORGE BERNARD SHAW, PLAYWRIGHT

Did you know that there are companies that will give you a loan of twenty-five hundred dollars, despite your credit history, if you simply send them a thirty-nine-dollar processing fee? Did you know you can buy ostrich chicks, raise them, and then sell the meat and hides for big profits? Did you know that an abundance of stocks sell for right around five dollars per share that you can buy, sell in six weeks, and double or triple your money? If you'd bite on any of these offers, you'd be contributing to the lifestyle improvement of a con artist.

Con artists perpetrate all sorts of scams and prey on anyone who has money. If you invest in stocks, whether you're a novice or a seasoned investor, you're prey to con artists. And the size of your wallet is insignificant. Some con artists prefer to target the fat portfolios of a few wealthy investors, while others set their sights on a larger number of smaller investors who have limited means. As far as the con artist is concerned, everyone's money spends the same. Whether you're an attorney, electrician, movie star, doctor, business executive, plumber, or economist is irrelevant to the con artist.

You can lose money to a scam without being an investor. If you borrow money, you may fall prey to advance fee loan fraud, in which the perpetrator illegally charges you a fee in return for a loan. If you use a credit card, you may have your identity stolen and your credit rating ruined. If you own a company, you may be the victim of your own employees or vendors. If you use the Internet, you may be scammed right in your own home.

No one really knows for sure how much money is lost to fraud each year, but it's in the billions of dollars and increases each year. The number of complaints and inquiries received by the New York Attorney General's Bureau of Investor Protection increased by 40 percent from 1995 to 1996 and another 40 percent from 1996 to 1997. And that's just one state!

One of the primary reasons for this rampant growth in fraud is Wall Street's bull market. The Dow Jones Industrial Average's rise from 4,000 in 1995 to 11,000 in 1999 was big news. It was reported in newspapers, magazines, and on the nightly news and talked about by people who had never even been interested in the stock market before. More people today than ever before are aware of the stock market and are investing for the first time. In fact, one in three U.S. households currently invests in securities as compared to only one in seventeen households in 1980. According to the Investment Company Institute, the number of mutual funds in existence grew from 2,715 with $810.3 billion in assets in 1988 to 7,058 mutual funds with $5.045 trillion in assets ten years later. Most U.S. workers have access to a 401(k) plan, a Keogh, or an Individual Retirement Account. With market returns exceeding 25 percent per year, these investors have become conditioned to larger-than-ever returns. That makes it easier for a con artist to convince a potential victim that an investment can generate a 30, 40, or 50 percent return within a short period of time.

You may be surprised to find out that most of these con artists are never put out of business. Because of the time and resources required to bring a criminal case against a con artist, very few are prosecuted for criminal offenses. The ones who are prosecuted are those who have stolen millions and millions of dollars or who have blazed a new path in the area of fraud by doing something outrageous and bringing a great deal of attention to themselves.

Others are disciplined by having their brokerage licenses in a specific state revoked, being fined, or being informed that the authorities are watching them. Those consequences, however, don't stop them. They don't care who's watching; a fine just means they need to raise more money in their next scam, and a revoked state license means they'll either work in another state where they do have a license, or they'll simply work without a license.

State securities agencies are stretched to the limit in terms of finances and personnel. It would be impossible for them to prosecute every case, and even if they did, the jails tend to be reserved for violent criminals rather than white-collar criminals. Recovery of lost funds in cases that are prosecuted is rare because the con artist has spent or hidden the money. At most, victims often receive just pennies on the dollar. Therefore, the chances that the victim of a scam will see the perpetrator in court and get some sort of satisfaction through the justice system are small.

We tend to be a nation of gamblers who want to get rich by picking the right numbers in the lottery or hitting the jackpot in a casino. That was made clear in July 1998 when the Powerball lottery produced the biggest jackpot ever—$295 million to a single winning ticket. Although the odds of winning were one in eighty million, people nevertheless drove to the borders of the states that had tickets for sale, causing major traffic jams. People stood in line for up to three hours to buy a ticket. Millions of people bought tickets, but only one ticket won.

Few of us will hit a major lottery jackpot. Instead, we need to focus on earning our money through hard work and wise investments. We need to know how to protect our money and understand that the only assurance we have of not being defrauded is our own knowledge, skepticism, and ability to recognize a scam. The following chapters look at the various types of fraud that exist today, give you tips on how to avoid becoming a victim, and offer you advice on what to do if you are defrauded.

At the end of each of the following chapters is a checklist of questions pertaining to the chapter's topic that you can ask yourself to determine if you may be dealing with a con artist, have become the potential victim of a fraud, or are on the right track to protecting yourself. Regardless of the type of fraud that may be perpetrated against you, you can help to protect yourself if you do the following:

- Check out the salesperson, the company, and the investment or offer through the Better Business Bureau, your state's attorney general's office, your state's securities agency, or other appropriate agencies.
- Ask for and read written information that explains the investment or offer.
- Get the opinion of a trusted friend, relative, or adviser.
- Verify any claims a salesperson makes.
- Never give out personal numbers such as Social Security or bank account numbers.
- Never allow yourself to be rushed into making a decision.

Knowing how to recognize a con artist and a fraudulent offer and taking the time to check them out will help to keep you fraud free. Knowledge is power, and power is what you need to keep the con artists at bay.

John Moscow, Assistant District Attorney, New York County District Attorney's Office, New York, New York

There are legislative changes that could be made that would help reduce the amount of fraud that's perpetrated in this country. First, we should repeal the Capital Formation Act of 1996. That legislation took the power to bar the registration of people in the securities field away from the state securities regulators and centralized it with the Securities and Exchange Commission (SEC). But the SEC is woefully understaffed and underfunded. Let's repeal that bill and give that power back to the states.

Second, the SEC routinely files injunctions barring people from violating securities laws. Those people, however, often violate those injunctions and continue to break securities laws. When that happens, the SEC cannot prosecute for contempt. Instead, it has to file another injunction. But that's a waste of time because these people obviously violate injunctions. Let's give the SEC the right to seek contempt citations so its enforcement division has the ability to get a criminal remedy for failure to obey the courts. Those two changes would help tremendously.

When asked why he robbed banks, Willie Sutton responded, "That's where the money is." We currently have a lot of people in the securities industry with the same morals as Willie. While we certainly can't legislate morality, we can put laws in place that give the regulators the power they need to prosecute con artists. That would be a big step in helping to reduce crime. The integrity of the market is what makes our markets better than markets anywhere else in the world. We have to maintain that integrity, and we can do that only by ensuring the proper prosecution of those who violate our laws.

CHAPTER 2

You'll Find a Friend in Me:
Meet the Con Artists

I went to my mother and told her
I intended to commence a different life.
I asked for and obtained her blessing, and at once
I commenced the career of a robber.

TIBURCIO VASQUEZ, CALIFORNIA OUTLAW

Meet John Dantero. He stands six feet seven inches, is good-looking and smart by most standards, and is a real go-getter. When he was growing up in San Antonio, Texas, he was a basketball star at an all-boys' Catholic school and won a basketball scholarship to the University of Texas in Austin, where he earned a degree in dentistry. After graduation, he decided dentistry was boring. He also discovered he couldn't stand the smell of anesthesia, so he decided to change careers. He worked as a stockbroker for a few years until a neighbor introduced him to oil and gas limited partnerships, a typically expensive, private investment.

By the early 1980s, when he was just thirty-five years old, Dantero was selling oil and gas deals and had made enough money to buy a Rolls-Royce, several Cadillacs, a limousine with a chauffeur who was also his cook, and several fancy condominiums. He even hired his own public relations person to promote him. His success story appeared in countless magazine articles in which he claimed to be worth $10 million.

Dantero is a con man. With a cohort, he founded a company and started selling oil and gas deals. But after a couple years of operation, the SEC filed a civil suit against him for securities fraud. He was also indicted by a federal grand jury on more than forty counts of related felony charges. He and his partner were charged with using false and misleading information to con $8 million from more than two hundred people who invested in four oil and gas ventures. In addition, the court documents accused them of diverting between two and three million dollars of the money for their personal use, such as buying a villa in Acapulco, building a swimming pool, purchasing expensive cars and diamond watches, and even undergoing plastic surgery.

Dantero denied any criminal intent in the suits and claimed he was a victim of his business partner, a former minister who, according to court documents, had a cocaine addiction. He also placed part of the blame on the company geologist for making major mistakes in certain estimates about the oil wells.

Despite his claims of innocence, Dantero ended up spending time in prison—part of it at the same prison his father called home when Dantero was a child.

Why did his victims trust him and hand over their money? Because he was personable, confident, articulate, and, most of all, a good salesman. Those are the character traits that most swindlers share—and those are the traits all investors want in the person they invest with. No one wants to trust his or her money with someone who isn't friendly, can't speak intelligently, and doesn't generate a certain amount of confidence about the product he's selling.

The Prototypical Con Man

While there are all types of con men, most of them share several personality traits. Typically they're narcissistic, self-centered, and grandiose. They have feelings of entitlement; they think they're special and entitled to live a good life. If achieving that good life means they have to engage in deceptive, immoral, and illegal behavior, that's fine with them.

Another common denominator is that they all have a large ego. In fact, that's part of the reason they're able to swindle people.

If most of us considered swindling people, we might be deterred by the thought of going to prison. But that doesn't seem to bother these guys, because they have such big egos and think they're so smart that they'll never get caught. They're sometimes wrong.

When they are caught, however, they typically deny having any part in the swindle. They always claim it's someone else's fault or they didn't really understand what was happening, or they were a victim of someone else, such as a business partner. In fact, each chapter in this book features an interview conducted with someone who is an expert on that chapter's topic. Finding con artists to interview was difficult. I spoke to several people who had spent years in prison for various types of fraud, but none of them would agree to be interviewed for the book, because they claimed they were innocent. So why did they do time in prison? They were framed, they said, or caught up in a misunderstanding, or were a victim of the system. Interestingly enough, these con artists I spoke to who claimed to be innocent were more than willing to give me the names of other con artists who they *knew* were guilty. Of course, when I called these sources, I found that they were also "innocent." After speaking to several con artists, I was finally able to find a couple who were willing to admit to their dark pasts.

Another trait many con artists share is the lack of a conscience or remorse. If they don't believe it's their fault and they blame someone else, why should they have remorse? They were just doing their job.

The Business of Con Men

Con men's business is getting money from other people. Once they get the money, they view it as theirs, regardless of what they might have promised to anyone. If the deal doesn't work or the business fails, their victim is out of luck. After all, he or she is the one who decided to take the risk.

Most scam artists know that what they're doing is a scam. They are the "take the money and run" guys. In fact, some are downright blatant about it.

Several years back, a group of teenagers leased an office, set up desks and phones, and started calling senior citizens, selling them oil and gas deals. They raised more than a quarter of a million dollars, which they used to purchase Corvettes and at least one home. When they'd make a call to a senior citizen and complete a sale, they'd slam down the phone and start laughing and talking about how they reeled in another sucker. But they hadn't realized that they had hired an honest secretary, who went to the state securities board and told the authorities the whole story. This was a swindle from the start.

Not all scams, however, start out as scams. Someone with good intentions may start a business and raise money from investors. But he ends up spending the money on items that may not pertain to the business, or the business simply may not work out. For whatever reason, he runs into money problems and in desperation uses whatever means he can to raise more funds. That probably includes lying about inflated revenues and profits, manufacturing false contracts and customers, and stealing any way he can. Eventually everything collapses. Either the authorities move in, or the con artist takes whatever money is available and runs with it.

A con artist's mind-set can be difficult to judge, which makes it hard for prosecutors. In a criminal case, prosecutors have to show that the scam was intentional from the beginning. The law says the con artist had to have the intent and knowledge that it was a scam at the time of the sale to the victim. But often it's hard to prove that the person planned to scam people from the outset.

While these people may be persuasive, have large egos, be somewhat flamboyant, and have no remorse, the good news is that they typically aren't violent. These are white-collar criminals, not street thugs. Of course, that doesn't mean you should push them. When confronted with detection and a prison sentence, anyone could become violent.

So Why Do They Do It?

It seems that putting together a scam would be a lot of hard work, so why not just get a legitimate job, work hard, and not worry about prison? The answer is money. Many con artists don't have a college education and have bad credit and money problems. Getting a legitimate job and making a lot of money is difficult for them. But if they put together a good scam, they can make a couple of hundred thousand dollars a year—enough to live an upper-middle-class (or better) lifestyle. If they don't think they'll get caught, and swindling people out of their money doesn't bother them, it's a great living.

Even if a swindler does get caught and spends time in prison, he may not turn honest when he's released. Obviously rehabilitation doesn't work if the person isn't interested in being rehabilitated. If a con artist decides to live by stealing money from victims, he'll continue his ways until he finally just burns out. Of course, some con artists claim to have seen the light and say they've been rehabilitated.

Can You Spot a Con Artist?

Although experts tell us that most con artists share a few common characteristics, there is no defining factor that tells you if someone is a swindler. It's possible that in conversation with a con artist, a psychologist may be able to detect a sense of insincerity, shallowness, and superficiality, but those tip-offs can be very difficult for the average person to pinpoint, as evidenced by the amount of fraud successfully perpetrated. If only con artists were all green, glowed in the dark, or had a special imprint on their foreheads, it would make life easier for all of us. But they don't. Some wear suits and ties, and some wear sweatshirts and jeans. They may be loud and brash, or soft-spoken and kind. Some who work out of sparse back rooms are only a voice over the phone. Others work from richly appointed offices and happily invite their prey into their lair. They may have an impressive array of letters behind their names. They'll be persuasive and know how to break down your resistance and convince you to hand over your money.

A Male Profession

You may have noticed that the word *he* has been used throughout to describe the con artist. According to Jules Burstein, a clinical and forensic psychologist from Berkeley, California, who works with con artists, that pronoun is correct. He believes that between 90 and 95 percent of all con artists are male. He attributes this to the fact that women as a group tend to be much more concerned about people's feelings and are more often hesitant to hurt others.

Women are also deterred by the possibility of going to prison and being separated from their children. If a woman is involved in a scam, she's typically not the ringleader, but is being used by her male counterpart. Male con artists, on the other hand, are typically much less concerned about losing access to their children, believe they can deal with incarceration, and have no remorse or feelings for their victims.

Although a lot of con men follow in their father's footsteps, Burstein doesn't believe that this behavior is genetic, but rather that it's social learning. For instance, if a boy sees his father being physically abusive to his mother during his childhood, that type of behavior becomes acceptable to him. There's more of a chance that that child will grow up to be an abusive partner than if he had not viewed domestic violence as a child. It's the same with crime. If a child sees a parent swindling other people and often getting away with it, as an adult that child will be much more inclined to consider engaging in that same type of behavior. Chances are, that behavior will last for some time, unless the individual wishes to change or burns out. The next generation may be at great risk for engaging in the same kind of deviant behavior.

Because trying to ascertain whether someone is legitimate or is a con artist is difficult, we have to use care and common sense in determining with whom we do business. We have to remember to take the time to check out any investment offers and the people who offer them. The con artist wants your money as badly as you do, and he doesn't care about you. His only concern is finding a way to continue his fraudulent behavior so he can live an extravagant lifestyle or maybe fund expensive habits such as gambling. As the old saying goes, possession is nine-tenths of the law. As long as you hold on to your money, it's yours; as soon as you hand it over, you may lose it forever.

Brett Champion, President,
Champion Entertainment, Beverly Hills, California

Sentenced to five years, probation in 1983 for mail fraud (first conviction)

Sentenced to five years, probation in 1990 for mail fraud (second conviction)

Sentenced to four years in federal prison in 1994 for wire fraud
(third conviction)

Served three years in federal prison

When I was fifteen, I started working the phones selling office
supplies two hours a day before school for a fraudulent telemarketing company. We promised people low prices and gifts for
placing orders. But there were no gifts, and the prices were actually exorbitant. I was making two to three thousand dollars a
week in commissions. That's when I realized I had a gift: I was
able to convince people that I was telling the truth and get them
to send me money without their investigating any of the facts.

In 1983, I was convicted of a fraudulent billing scheme in
which I billed corporations for products and services they didn't
receive. A large percentage of the companies paid the bogus
bills, and I made millions. All I got for that was five years' probation—basically a slap on the hand. In 1990, I was convicted of
running an illegal sports information, gambling, and betting service. Again, I made millions. I got another five years' probation.
In 1994, I was convicted of wire fraud. I had been selling investments in oil wells and told people their investment of twenty-five
thousand dollars would be worth a million dollars by the end of
the year. I took in ten million dollars within twenty-four months.
But the only place the oil wells existed was in my head. For that
crime I was finally sentenced to four years in federal prison. That
was my wake-up call.

After I was in jail a week, I knew that if I had been sent to
prison for my first offense, I never would have committed
another crime. In prison you lose your freedom, your family;
you're locked up, made a slave, and told what to do, what to
wear, what to eat. It was traumatic and devastating. Most con
artists have psychological problems or drug habits and keep reof-
fending, but I was able to rehabilitate myself while I was in
prison. I would never defraud anyone again.

I don't have any of the money I stole. All the assets from
my lavish lifestyle were seized when I was arrested, and the rest
of the money I had already gambled away. I now live in a small
apartment, drive a used American car, have no fancy jewelry or
any money in the bank. I live very modestly.

I currently operate my own fraud prevention company. I appear on television shows, speak at universities and to senior citizen groups, conduct seminars, and create law enforcement training tapes. I can't change what I did in the past, but I have turned my life around. Even though I went to prison and paid my debt to society, I've dedicated the rest of my life to helping people not become victims of fraud. The personal pleasure I get from that work is of greater satisfaction to me than I ever received from making all that money.

Checklist

Are you dealing with a salesperson who:

☐ Tends to be narcissistic and self-centered and has a large ego?

☐ Makes promises that no other salesperson can even come close to matching?

☐ Is very persuasive, convincing, and has the ability to break down your resistance slowly?

☐ Is unwilling to take no for an answer?

If you answered yes to any of these questions, you may be dealing with a con artist.

TARGETED VICTIMS

Ripping Off Our National Treasures: Elder Fraud

There is no safety for honest men but by believing all possible evil of evil men.

EDMUND BURKE, CONGRESSMAN

The following is an excerpt from an actual telephone conversation between a seventy-eight-year-old widow and a con artist who targets senior citizens. The conversation was recorded by the FBI and is used by the American Association of Retired Persons (AARP) Consumer Affairs Department in its fight against elder fraud. We're entering the conversation just after the con artist has told the woman that she won fifty thousand dollars, but before she can collect her prize, she has to pay two hundred and fifty dollars to cover certain fees.

Con artist:	You just relax. I'm going to take care of you, OK? You do know for a fact that the $250 will hold on your MasterCard. Correct?
Victim:	I think it would, but I'm not sure. I could send you a check.
Con artist:	No ma'am you can't. I swear to God, this is just crazy. Somebody spends all this money and wins $50,000 and you tell them what they have to do

	and they don't do it. Would your card cover $200?
Victim:	I'm not sure. I haven't gotten my statement.
Con artist:	OK. You're really not going to tell me, are you?
Victim:	I'm not sure. I'm telling you the truth. I'm not sure.
Con artist:	OK. Will it cover $100?
Victim:	It probably will, but I cannot. . . . I am 78 years old and it is dark. . . .
Con artist:	You're not going to go to the American Express [office] anyway, are you?
Victim:	I can't!
Con artist:	See, why didn't you just tell me that before I went through all this trouble. Let me just ask you something. I don't care if you're 78 or 88 or 108. You've got . . . I don't care what you've heard on the telephone. I don't care how badly you've been taken advantage of. I don't care if you hate me. You've got $50,000. That's the truth. I can go to bed living with the fact that I told you the truth and you were too stubborn or just refused to believe me and I had to pick another name and give it to somebody else. If I have to give it to somebody else, I'm going to. But I need some cooperation from you. And if I don't get it, you're hurting yourself. This is enough money for you to set up anybody you care about and go to your grave knowing that you went and did the right thing and you can go and meet God with a clear conscience. Now what do you want to do? Do you want your winnings or do you just want me to go ahead and just hang up the phone with you and forget that I ever saw your name?
Victim [*crying*]:	Of course I want the winnings, but I . . .
Con artist:	So now you're going to start crying again and going off on me, right? Do you want your money ma'am?
Victim:	Of course I do! Of course I do!
Con artist:	Now, will you cooperate?
Victim:	I'm trying to!

Pretty brutal, right? Brutality, harassment, and abuse are only a few of the techniques con artists employ when dealing with senior citizens.

The Targets

The telephone conversation that opens this chapter isn't an anomaly. It's replayed in homes across the nation every day. The Federal Bureau of Investigation (FBI) states that 80 percent of telemarketing calls are targeted at senior citizens. While senior citizens comprise about 36 percent of the U.S. adult population, it's estimated that they represent 56 percent of consumer fraud victims. And once they've become a victim, they will be called over and over because the con artists sell names of victims to each other in the black market. One name can bring as much as two hundred dollars.

And how did their name get on this list in the first place? The person may have entered a sweepstakes or a contest or ordered a bank card or subscribed to a magazine or become a member of an organization. Many companies and organizations sell their customers' names as a source of income.

The experience of being defrauded is devastating for a senior citizen. Senior citizens don't have the time or ability to work to replace lost funds. Many times, because of these frauds, their standard of living is severely affected. They may lose their home or be forced to sell it. Their families are also affected when they're called on to support a once self-supporting family member. These results are so physically and psychologically devastating that some victims have even become suicidal.

Con artists target senior citizens for several reasons:

- They have money. Senior citizens have been accumulating assets all their lives and have investments, real estate, and other assets stashed away.

- Senior citizens are reachable; they're at home during the day when the con artists are at work making calls.

- The elderly are polite and not inclined to hang up on someone or close the door on the person even though that person is invading their privacy. And the longer they listen, the more likely they are to agree to whatever the person is proposing.

- Seniors are trusting. They view this person as trying to make a living—much like their own children or grand-children.

- Many senior citizens live alone and are lonely and appreciate the opportunity to talk to someone.

- Senior citizen victims may become incapacitated and not be able to travel to the destinations required to testify if the con artist is caught. Or they may die before they can testify against the con artist or before the fraud is even detected. A Texas company targeting senior citizens in Texas, Florida, and Arizona convinced victims that their wills were inadequate or invalid and that a living trust and insurance annuities would solve the problem. They'd convince the senior citizen to tear up his or her will and buy a living trust from the con artist at a base price of $1,895. The average cost for a living will drawn up by an attorney is approximately $300 to $700. Many times, this fraud wasn't detected until the victim died and the heirs discovered the problem. In several cases, the validity of the living trusts was even questioned.

- Many widows left business dealings to their husbands. Now alone, they have to handle the finances, the investing, the home repair, and the auto maintenance. But they don't have the experience to know what is a good investment, what it should cost to have the house painted, or if the tires on the car really need to be rotated. They are easy prey.

- Older victims are often reluctant to report the crime to the authorities because they're embarrassed or afraid they'll be seen as incompetent and their children will take control over their affairs.

- Senior citizens are sometimes unable to recall the details of the fraud because it may have involved several phone calls or visits from the con artist over a long period of time. Without that information, it makes it more difficult for the authorities to prosecute.

- The con artists can wear down their victims with a marathon pitch until they simply give in from exhaustion. One Florida woman opened her door to a salesman who wanted to sell her a $2,985 medical alert system that she could wear around her neck and use to signal help if she couldn't get to a phone in the event of an emergency. After eight hours, the man was still in her home insisting that she buy his product. It was quarter to nine at night, and the woman was tired, hungry, and couldn't convince the salesman to leave. She wrote him a check.

The Scam

While con artists use all types of frauds against senior citizens, the AARP reports that the number one scam used most often is the offer of prizes, free gifts, and claims of winning a sweepstakes. The victims are told they can't collect their prizes until they send the con artist money for taxes, bonding, or registration. The truth is that if you have to pay, you haven't won, because it's illegal to require a person to pay money or purchase a good or service to collect a prize.

The con artist in this scam uses the tactic of excitement, because if he's excited, it gets the victim excited. How can anyone resist the booming voice coming over the phone that says, "Congratulations, this is your lucky day! You just won fifty thousand dollars!!"?

He'll also try to personalize his message. If your name is Mary, you'll hear the word *Mary* over and over during the conversation. He'll try to be familiar and have something in common with you. If you live in Florida, he'll say his mother lives in Florida and he just loves Florida. Or he may claim to have the same first name or same last name as yours, or he'll be a war veteran like you, or be of the same religion—anything that creates a connection.

He may try to create a relationship of reciprocity by doing you a favor, then asking you to pay back the favor. For example, he may say, "The fee is supposed to be one hundred dollars, but since we're both veterans of past wars and I like you, I'll reduce it to eighty dollars. But don't tell my boss I'm doing this." He's just done you a favor, and now he expects a favor in return: for you to accept the offer and send the eighty dollars.

He'll use high pressure and deceptive sales pitches to sell

you living trusts; low-risk, high-yield investments; arthritis remedies; work-at-home deals; rare coins; nonexistent oil well investments; overpriced medigap insurance; medical alert devices; and more. There's always an urgency to make a decision so you don't have time to check out the offer. He'll need your money immediately and may even offer to send a courier to pick it up.

He may try to make you think you're doing a good deed by accepting his offer. In 1997, American Publishers Exchange was required by the state of Nevada to pay fines totaling $369,000 for targeting senior citizens in a magazine sales scam. Victims were told that they would receive valuable prizes if they purchased a $489 magazine subscription. The prizes they received were not worth what the victims paid. To make matters worse, the victims were told if they paid an additional $1,400 to $3,000, the proceeds would go to an antidrug program for children. Of course, the money went in the con artist's pocket.

If sheer lies don't work, the con artist will often revert to abuse. The phone conversation at the beginning of this chapter employed the tactic of abuse, but that's nothing compared to the badgering some con artists employ. They may scream, use obscenities, and belittle you.

The con artist is happy to target any senior citizen, but most people envision the stereotypical victim to be a senior citizen who lives alone, is not very sophisticated, is naive, and is basically a lonely recluse. Not so. A 1997 AARP survey, in which 745 victims of elder fraud were interviewed found that the typical victims of elder fraud are well educated, fairly sophisticated, and active in community activities. Most of the victims, however, didn't envision the con artist as a criminal and therefore were willing to listen to his pitch. A few even told the people conducting the survey that they liked to go to Las Vegas, liked to play bingo, and enjoyed taking a risk and getting some fun out of it. They viewed the con artist's phone call in the same light. Unfortunately, the odds of winning when dealing with a con artist are much lower than those in Las Vegas or in a bingo hall.

Con artists also use the recovery room tactic on senior citizens, in which they call their previous victims and offer to help them get their money back for a small fee. As soon as the victim sends in the fee, he or she never hears from the caller again.

Although the phone is the primary tool con artists use to reach their prey, it isn't the only way. A senior citizen's mailbox may be stuffed every day with fraudulent claims and come-ons. Post-cards tell them they've won prizes. Letters try to convince them to send money to an unscrupulous charity. Brochures try to sell them merchandise that isn't worth its cost.

Sometimes the con artists come right to the door. They may be dressed as policemen or firemen with realistic badges and IDs claiming to be collecting money for their departments. They may be workers who offer to resurface the driveway, paint the house, or repair the roof. They complete the job quickly, do poor-quality work, and charge a much higher amount than they initially quoted, which was already higher than the going rate. In some cases, they demand advance payment for materials and then dis-appear. Or they may begin tearing up the driveway, start stripping the paint, or begin removing shingles, and then demand more money to finish the job.

Protecting Yourself From Elder Fraud

No senior citizen has to become a victim of fraud. By taking a few precautions and not letting greed overcome common sense, you can be safe.

One of the first steps you should take is to remove your name from participating national telemarketing lists. You can do that by sending your name, address, phone number, and signature to:

Direct Marketing Association
Telephone Preference Service
P.O. Box 9014
Farmingdale, NY 11735-9014

To remove your name from participating national mailing lists, send your name, home address, and signature to:

Direct Marketing Association
Mail Preference Service
P.O. Box 9008
Farmingdale, NY 11735-9008

Both services are free, but there is a ninety-day processing period before you'll see a gradual reduction in phone calls and mail. Your name will stay on these lists for five years. If you need other information or want a preaddressed postcard sent to you that you can use as an application rather than having to send a letter, you can contact the Direct Marketing Association at 202-955-5030. Everyone should take advantage of this service.

Making these requests will reduce the calls and mail you receive, but it may not stop the con artists. They don't care that the law says they can't call you or mail solicitations to you. Despite their unwillingness to adhere to the law, you should still take these steps because if they hound you after you've signed up with the Direct Marketing Association, pressing charges against them is easier. If you want more information on how to deal with solicitors, call the National Fraud Information Center (NFIC) at 1-800-876-7060 and ask for brochures that offer guidelines on avoiding and dealing with fraud.

If you are faced with dealing with con artists, the best defense you can mount is to be ready for them:

- Be prepared and have a message in mind you can use.
- Tell them you have no money.
- Tell them you don't do business with strangers over the phone.
- Tell them you're simply not interested and hang up.
- If you choose to talk to them and listen to their pitch, don't get pressured into making a quick decision.
- Always ask for written information, including the company's refund policy.
- Talk to a friend or trusted adviser, and get that person's opinion of the offer.
- Call the Better Business Bureau and your state attorney general's office and ask if any complaints have been made against the company.
- Never send money to anyone you don't know, and never reveal personal numbers such as your credit card, Social Security, or bank account numbers.

Remember that these con artists are professional liars. If they tell you you've won a contest, think back. Do you remember entering the contest? Chances are you never did, because the contest doesn't exist. If someone rings your doorbell and wants to resurface your driveway, why would you say yes if you hadn't even been considering having your driveway resurfaced? If you're asked to give money to a charity, ask the purpose of the charity, the programs and services it provides, what percentage of the donation goes to expenses and salaries, if the charity is registered in your state; then request the annual report. If you want to give money to your local fire or police department, do it locally and in person.

When you need repairs done to your home, get bids from several contractors and check their reputation with the Better Business Bureau, through references, or through your local building inspector's office. Always get a written contract outlining the work to be done and the amount to be paid. Never pay for all the work up front.

Through legislation, the authorities are working to keep con artists from plying their trade. The Federal Trade Commission has regulations that every salesperson must follow. When someone calls you, they're required to identify their company's name and tell you what they're selling. They cannot require you to pay for a prize or to pay for services in advance. Solicitors aren't allowed to call you before 8:00 A.M. or after 9:00 P.M. your local time.

The government is taking steps specifically to protect senior citizens. In 1994, a statute was passed that provides for an additional ten years' imprisonment for some federal telemarketing schemes if the con artists targeted people who were over fifty-five years of age or victimized more than ten people over the age of fifty-five.

The key to stopping elder fraud lies with senior citizens. By refusing to deal with con artists on the phone, at their door, or through the mail, they'll be able to stay fraud free. It can be difficult to do. Anyone would hate to pass up the deal of a lifetime when it's offered, but the deal of a lifetime may be the deal that destroys the victim's life emotionally, physically, and psychologically. To ensure that doesn't happen to the senior citizens who are near and dear to our hearts, each of us should take time to encourage them to pass by any temptations presented to them. The line we preach to our children should be the same line we preach to our national treasures—our senior citizens: Just Say No!!!

Bridget Small, Leader of the Telemarketing Fraud Team, American Association of Retired Persons, Washington, D.C.

If you have elderly family members or friends you're concerned about, there are red flags you can watch for to determine if they've become the victim of a fraud. Do they receive an excessive number of phone calls, get an excessive amount of mail, or have a lot of purchases or prize giveaway trinkets such as pens lying around the house? Do they receive multiple copies of magazines or videos? Are they making payments to out-of-state companies or are private courier services coming to their homes to pick up payments? Do they have lists of registration numbers or phone numbers to call in connection with sweepstakes?

Even if you do not see any red flags in a senior citizen's home, have a conversation about the possibility of fraud, and in a nonthreatening way. If you're accusatory and the senior citizen is involved in a fraud, he or she may not tell you if you come on too strong. Open the conversation neutrally with a statement such as, "I get lots of junk mail and lots of calls from people trying to give me a prize or sell me something. Do you?"

How you deal with a parent or relative on their handling of potentially fraudulent offers is a sensitive issue. If your parents want to spend their money on certain items, that's their prerogative. You can't ban what they do, but at the same time, you want to protect them.

If you suspect your loved one has become a victim of fraud, call the state attorney general or secretary of state. The phone numbers can be found in the government pages of the phone book. Certainly you want to give your loved ones the freedom to do as they please, but you also need to protect them from professional con artists. You can do that by paying attention to what they're doing, talking to them about potential frauds, and making sure they understand the real risks that lurk outside their door, in their mailbox, and at the end of their phone line. Everyone should take steps to ensure that senior citizens remain fraud free.

Checklist

Does the person:

- ❏ Refuse to take no for an answer?
- ❏ Ask you to send money before collecting a prize or gift?
- ❏ Pressure you to make a decision immediately?
- ❏ Request a fee to help you recover money lost from a previous scam?
- ❏ Use harassment and abuse to bully you into sending money?
- ❏ Appear at your door wanting you to hire him to do repairs around your home?

If you answered yes to any of these questions and you're a senior citizen, you're dealing with a con artist who probably targets senior citizens.

CHAPTER 4

You and Me—We're Alike: Affinity Fraud

Love your enemies in case your friends turn out to be a bunch of bastards.

R. A. DICKSON

Once there was a unique grocery store in Houston. It was called Fiesta—just like a party! Fiesta, which catered to Hispanics, was more than a grocery store. Included on its property were other retail outlets such as a travel agency, an optical shop, and a jewelry store. In the midst of all these shops, and right next to Fiesta's customer service booth, was a company called Moneytron.

We've all heard the saying that if it looks like a duck, walks like a duck, and quacks like a duck, it's probably a duck. Right? Well, Moneytron looked like a bank, acted like a bank, and the employees all talked as if they were running a bank. So it must be a bank. Right? We'll get to that later.

The owners of Moneytron were Hispanic, as were the employees. That made the customers, primarily Hispanic, very comfortable. Although many were not in their native country, they could do business with people from their own country—people who shared the same culture and background. Plus, Moneytron catered to their unique needs. Stacked on the countertops at Moneytron were new account forms, printed in English and Spanish, that customers could fill out to open a savings account. And the best part was that the customers didn't have to have a Social Security number to open an account, so illegal immigrants could have savings accounts. No other bank offered them that option. The other special service Moneytron offered was to transfer money to their customers' countries of origin for them.

Everything worked fine as long as the customers kept making deposits. But in the late 1980s, the U.S. government granted amnesty to groups of illegal immigrants who met certain qualifications. Suddenly a lot of illegals were no longer illegal, and they could apply for a Social Security number. With that Social Security number, they could open savings accounts and checking accounts at any bank. When they began withdrawing their funds from Moneytron, a problem quickly cropped up: Moneytron didn't have nearly enough money to pay the depositors. The reality was that despite its appearance, Moneytron was not a bank at all. It was not federally insured, and it was run by people who were stealing the money. By the time anyone realized what was happening, hundreds of depositors had been defrauded, to the tune of more than $1 million.

This story, however, has an ending that isn't typical in fraud cases. Even though the depositors' money was gone, the authorities, in a civil suit against Fiesta, won damages that were sufficient to more than compensate the victims for their losses—a rare "everyone lived happily ever after" ending to this fraud.

This type of fraud is called *affinity fraud*. The dictionary defines the word *affinity* as "a close relationship, a connection, or a common origin." The connection of being Hispanic and understanding a specific need of those in the community is the connection that Moneytron promoters used to lure their victims.

Targets of Affinity Fraud

Ethnic affinity fraud runs rampant in the United States because there's such a large pool of potential victims. In 1996, 915,900 immigrants from countries around the world came into the United States by legal means, a 27 percent increase from 1995. Others entered the country by illegal means, but no one knows how many. When it comes to ethnic affinity fraud, the nationalities that con artists most typically target are Hispanics, African Americans, Asians, and Indians, although no one is immune from being the target of a con artist.

Affinity fraud also goes beyond ethnic groups. Any group that has a connection or relationship where the con artist can become a part of that group can be targeted. Churches and their congregations are often swindled by one of their own members who has joined the church, made friends with parishioners, and gained their trust. In some cases, even the ministers can't be trusted.

Self-proclaimed Pentecostal minister Wendell J. Rogers, who was also the director and CEO of Sunbelt Development Corporation, conned fellow pastors and members of their congregations in four states into investing millions of dollars in an investment scam. He told his victims he was a wealthy, licensed securities broker whose area of expertise was in arranging short-term bridge loans at high interest rates. By investing with him, he said, they could earn as much as a 50 percent return per year. Since he was a pastor, everyone believed him. But rather than investing the money in legitimate business ventures, Rogers pocketed the money, using a portion of it to purchase a Rolls-Royce.

Affinity fraud exists in the workplace too. If you work side by side with someone every day, you'll probably get to know that person fairly well and eventually come to trust him. That's what happened when an Indiana factory worker convinced his co-workers that, despite his working on an assembly line, he had a net worth of more than thirty million dollars. He swore he could invest their money in companies and partnerships that would give them a 30 percent return per month. He was able to convince his co-workers to invest more than $160,000 with him. Unfortunately, the companies and partnerships he was touting never existed.

Affinity fraud works because people feel comfortable dealing with someone they think is like them and presumably shares the same beliefs, culture, or background. We have a tendency to trust our own. Many immigrants don't understand how the financial markets work in this country. Many Americans don't know how to research an investment. These people turn to one of their own countrymen, a fellow church member, or a coworker who purports to be an expert.

How the Con Works

In affinity fraud, the first step for the con artist is to identify himself with the group. He'll point out his ethnicity, become a church member, take a job where he can work side by side with his intended victims, or become a trusted financial adviser to members of a specific profession, such as teachers or doctors. Typically he'll begin with one or two prominent people in the group who tend to be leaders and convince them to invest. If the group leaders bite, the con artist uses their names when trying to convince others to invest, giving him more credibility. In many cases, con artists have even won over the minister or pastor of a church, who then encourages parishioners, sometimes even in the Sunday sermons, to invest their money with this person.

Affinity fraud encompasses all types of other fraud. Once the con artist has won the trust of the group, the fraud perpetrated may be a high-tech scheme, an Internet swindle, commodity fraud, or any other type of scam. But the main focus of affinity fraud is for the con artist to become part of the group and earn the people's trust to the extent that they feel comfortable with him, believe in him, and are willing to hand their money over to him.

Protecting Yourself From Affinity Fraud

To avoid becoming a victim of affinity fraud, don't accept advice from another person just because you share the same ancestry or race, hold the same beliefs, or have other common characteristics such as working together or being members of the same organization. Phrases like "You can trust me; we have to stick together" or "You and I are alike" shouldn't be enough to convince you to hand over your money.

Beware also of testimonials from members of your group. Others may have invested with this person and received the high returns they were promised, but if the con artist is running a swindle, those returns may have come from money other people invested. Even if early investors got their expected returns, they are still victims of affinity fraud. Chances are that no one else will reap any benefits.

When approached with any kind of investment, always get a prospectus or other written information that details what the investment is, how it works, its risks, and how you cash out of the investment. Ask a trusted professional—your accountant, attorney, or financial adviser—to review the written materials, explain them to you, and give you his opinion. Be sure that trusted professional is someone who is an uninterested third party and not connected with your group. And always check out the person and company offering the investment with your state securities agency or the Better Business Bureau.

If, despite your care you find you've been scammed, report it to your state securities agency. Part of the reason that fraud is so rampant is that victims don't report it; therefore, con artists continue to defraud others.

Affinity fraud is especially cruel because it plays on people's trust and loyalty to one another. Suddenly people find they can't trust those who are closest to them—co-workers, fellow parishioners, even clergy. Not only do you lose your money with affinity fraud, but you lose your feelings of trust for others. Affinity fraud can cause you to become skeptical, untrusting, and cynical. Most of us don't want to go through life with those feelings, but a small dose of those characteristics may just keep us from falling prey to this type of fraud.

Pastor Jonathan Saffold Sr., Ebenezer Church of God in Christ, Milwaukee, Wisconsin

Being in the inner city, we always look forward to being a part of a business that is new and innovative. We were given that opportunity in 1997 when a church member suggested we invest in a new company that offered local and long-distance telephone service. The company was to buy the service wholesale and sell it retail. The man starting the company had been active in the community, had been a member of the church, and had a good rapport with everybody, and we trusted him.

As I understood it, we were promised that at a minimum, as a conservative estimate, the money we put in would be worth ten times its value within one year. The company would then go public, and we'd make even more money. One of our other church members is a very successful businessman, and he was convinced that this new phone company was a good deal. My wife and I invested $10,500.

The company was in business from spring 1997 to August or September—about six months. In the end, we found out that the company's bills had not been paid; in fact, the company did not even have a legitimate license to operate. As I understood, this guy had started two or three companies, but only one had a license, and he used that one license illegally for all the companies. He had created a national company and a state company with a network marketing company tied in, and one was doing business through another. It was so mixed up that it looked as if the whole thing was a scam from the beginning.

We lost all our money. It really hurts to have a friend let you down like that. You want to kick yourself for not investigating the investment and being more selective, but that's hindsight. I look at the lost money as tuition toward a course in how not to lose money. The worst thing you can do is to get so sour over an incident like this that you can't function. I'm an optimistic person, and I don't think people should give up investing because of a mistake. This is the land of the free and the land of opportunity, and it would be a shame not to invest in it.

You just have to be a wise investor, check out everything before you commit, and if the investment doesn't stand up to tough scrutiny, don't invest. It's better to pass up a specific investment and not make money than to invest and lose money.

Checklist

Does the person:

- ❑ Encourage you to trust him simply because you have a connection such as race, ancestry, or being members of the same organization?

- ❑ Want you to invest with him based purely on your connection?

❑   Focus on gaining the trust of the leader of your group before approaching others

❑   Flaunt testimonials from members of your group?

If you answered yes to any of these questions, you may be the targeted victim of affinity fraud.

PART THREE

THE OLD AND THE NEW

CHAPTER 5

The Old Standbys: Ponzis and Pyramids

If you rob Peter to pay Paul, you can always count on Paul's support.

ANONYMOUS

The two cons we look at in this chapter, Ponzi and pyramid schemes, have been around for a while and will continue to be a popular choice with con artists. Understand the characteristics of each type of scheme so you can recognize it when it presents itself. Stay one step ahead of the con artist, be skeptical, always trust your instincts, and beat him at his own game.

Ponzi Schemes

In the world of con artists, it must be a real honor to have a swindle named after you. So it is with the ageless Ponzi schemes that seem to be as popular today as they became in 1919 when an Italian immigrant, Charles Ponzi, moved to Boston and dreamed up the first one. The backdrop of his scheme was international postal reply coupons (IPRCs), which could be redeemed for stamps in other countries.

Ponzi realized that by purchasing IPRCs in a country whose currency was weak, he could redeem them for stamps in a country whose currency was strong and make a small profit on the differing rates of exchange. He found that he could purchase Spanish IPRCs for a penny and redeem them in the United States for ten cents. Ponzi had that old con artist instinct in him and decided that if he could get other people to invest in his scheme, he could turn his small profit into a big profit.

He began soliciting money from investors who were typically earning about a 5 percent return with other types of investments and promised them a 40 percent return in just three months. The earliest investors did indeed receive their 40 percent return, but the money Ponzi used to pay that return came from the money later investors were putting into the deal—*not* from the purchase and sale of IPRCs. The truth was that it would have been impossible for the money to come from the purchase and sale of IPRCs. That's because IPRCs were issued only for the convenience of postal customers who used international mail, so the number issued was very limited. In fact, fewer than one million dollars' worth of these coupons had ever been issued by the Spanish government. The orders that Ponzi received were so huge that he never could have purchased enough IPRCs to cover them, but that didn't stop him. In fact, he began promising investors even higher returns: 50 percent in ninety days, and eventually even more.

When the authorities learned of the swindle, they exposed it through the newspapers. But people didn't believe the authorities and continued to send money to Ponzi. When the swindle was shut down, investors blamed the Massachusetts authorities for victimizing Ponzi and ruining their chances of getting their money back with a huge return. In the end, Ponzi stole ten million dollars from forty thousand Bostonians. Throughout the whole caper, Ponzi purchased less than fifty dollars' worth of IPRCs.

The classic Ponzi scheme is still popular today and works in the same way. The promoter of a Ponzi scheme offers huge returns to investors in a "can't-lose" money-making scheme. To give the appearance that this is a legitimate investment, the promoter pays off the earliest investors, but with the money he collects from later investors. Those first investors, who receive their 50 or 60 percent return, begin to brag about this great investment they made. When others hear, they want to invest and make those same returns, so the promoter collects even more money. The scheme collapses when the number of previous investors looking for a return exceeds the number of new investors available to fuel the scheme with new money. At that point, the promoter bolts with the money he has taken in, leaving the investors with their losses. A Ponzi scheme can be tied to any type of business—such as gold mines, finance companies, designer jeans, diamonds, or cosmetics, but in fact— as with most swindles, the underlying business becomes secondary to the promoter.

Often a Ponzi scheme starts out by targeting a specific group, such as members of a church, residents of a particular area, military personnel at a specific base, or people in the entertainment industry. Demographics are important to the Ponzi scheme because the con artist has to depend on news of his great investment spreading by word of mouth to find new investors. Therefore, he needs a homogeneous group in which the members have access to each other so they can spread the word. The demographics of a Ponzi scheme can be large. If the promoter starts out targeting members of a specific church, the church members who invest will tell their friends, and word will spread beyond the church. And word can spread quickly.

In 1998, the authorities shut down a Ponzi scheme in which the promoter was raising money to develop a national chain of upscale golf and entertainment centers. The scheme had originated in central Florida but had already spread across fifteen states by the time the authorities stepped in. The promoters had raised $16.5 million. The authorities reported that about one million dollars of the money was used to pay returns to early investors, and the rest of the money was used for operating expenses, sales commissions, and lavish lifestyles for the promoters.

Ponzi schemes always offer an economic purpose so that investors think they are investing in a viable venture that generates income, such as offering mortgages, selling oil and gas leases, or making loans to small businesses. The promoters usually have glossy brochures and names of satisfied customers they use as references.

A good Ponzi scheme can last for years. The people who get in early are earning the high profits they were promised, and they are often so excited about the investment that not only do they tell their friends, but they reinvest the money they've received back from the investment and sometimes invest additional funds. It's difficult for authorities to convince victims to cooperate when the scheme is uncovered, because they don't want it to collapse. Unfortunately, they don't think about the people who are just beginning to invest, who will, without question, lose their money.

Ponzi schemes are some of the largest types of scams that exist in terms of dollars stolen. Victims who worked for forty years to build a retirement nest egg have ended up losing it in these schemes. Not only are the financial results devastating to the victims, but so are the physical and mental consequences.

In the past, authorities didn't focus on white-collar crimes, so con artists didn't have much to fear. Authorities now pay more attention to white-collar crime. Because of the size of the losses in Ponzi schemes and the impact those losses have on the victims, the promoters of Ponzi schemes now draw some of the longest prison sentences of any type of con artist. For example, a promoter who was indicted in San Antonio for a fifty-million-dollar Ponzi scheme was given a ten-year prison sentence. A promoter who took fifty-eight million dollars from three thousand investors was sentenced to sixteen years in prison. Another promoter, who stole ten million dollars by running a Ponzi scheme that operated under the guise of a bank, was sentenced to twelve years in prison. Even with stiff prison sentences, however, you can be sure that the classic scam Charles Ponzi dreamed up eighty years ago will continue to thrive.

Protecting Yourself From Ponzi Schemes

As with any other type of fraud, you are your own best line of defense. Use common sense and invest only after you've done your homework and checked out an investment, as follows:

- Invest only with legitimate, licensed brokers; if you have trouble with the broker, the firm is responsible. If the person is not licensed, find out why.
- Obtain and read the investment prospectus. Get all the facts in writing. Be sure you understand the offer and that it fits your investment objectives. If it isn't clear to you, ask a trusted adviser to read it. If it isn't clear to the adviser, it isn't worth investing in.
- Verify any claims the promoter makes. If he says the offering

is registered with a governmental agency or that it has the endorsement of a specific organization, check it out.

- Call the state securities agency, the Better Business Bureau, and other reliable sources to check out the company and the person to be sure both are legitimate. If investors had checked out Charles Ponzi's background, they would have found that he was a con artist who had been sentenced to three years in the penitentiary for forgery and another two years in prison for violation of immigration laws.

- If the offer involves a company that produces a product, visit the plant where the product is made. Don't fall for the excuse that the plant is under renovation or is off-limits due to security concerns. It may be off-limits to you because it doesn't exist.

- Never invest in get-rich-quick schemes that offer guaranteed high profits. Remember that the higher the return an investment pays, the higher the level of risk is. Also, don't consider investments in which you're encouraged to put your profits back into the investment.

- If the promoters don't return your phone calls or don't answer your questions before you invest, think how bad it will be after you invest. If they act unprofessionally, don't invest.

Pyramid Schemes

The classic pyramid scheme originated in the late 1960s with Koscot Interplanetary's Glen Turner and his Dare to Be Great scheme. Investors paid five thousand dollars for the opportunity to sell mink oil cosmetics or to attend self-motivation seminars. Then they made money by selling cosmetics or recruiting others to buy distributorships for selling the cosmetics or the seminars. Because the company provided practically no advertising or assistance with product distribution for selling the cosmetics, most investors chose to recoup their money by bringing in new recruits. At revival-type meetings, Turner would promise investors great riches. The scheme collapsed after thousands of people lost more than forty million dollars. Investors sued Turner, and he was prosecuted, but the pyramid scheme was born, and others quickly developed.

Unlike a Ponzi scheme, which is a passive investment, a pyramid is a business the investor can buy in to and run. The investor is given the opportunity to buy in to the company, giving her the ability to sell a product such as magazine subscriptions, gold coins, or telephones. But in truth, the product has little value and really isn't important to the overall scheme. The primary focus of the pyramid is that the investor earns a commission for each person she recruits to become a salesperson.

Characteristics of a pyramid scheme include an opportunity in which investors are told they can make huge profits without doing much work. They're charged a membership fee to join; then they're expected to recruit other members, for whom they earn commissions. The products they were told they'd be selling become irrelevant; but even if they didn't, they'd be difficult to sell because they carry high price tags and are of low quality.

In some cases, the product is dispensed with completely. One popular pyramid scheme that had no product was the airplane game. New recruits would pay one hundred dollars and be designated a passenger on a nonexistent airplane. As they brought in other new recruits, their status would rise from passenger to flight crew, to copilot, and finally to pilot. When they became a pilot, they'd receive one thousand dollars or more.

On the surface, a pyramid scheme looks organized and businesslike, but it's typically almost impossible to make sense of the plan the promoters set forth in their marketing materials. Promoters target a defined group of people who may be seeking extra money or want a new career. They typically seek out people who may not be very sophisticated in finance and recruit closely-knit groups of people to increase the peer pressure to invest.

Pyramids don't exist for very long, because the number of people available to recruit quickly diminishes, and the pyramid withers away if regulators haven't already shut it down. In order for everyone to profit, there would have to be a never-ending supply of recruits. Consider how quickly the pool of new recruits can be depleted. If 7 people begin the pyramid and each one recruits 7 others, those original 7 people become 49 people. Those 49 people recruiting 7 people each become 343 people. By the time the pyramid reached the eighth level, there would be almost 6 million people, who would have to recruit more than 40 million more people for the pyramid to continue. The promoter knows there is a saturation point, and when he believes that point is close, he walks away with the money.

With pyramid schemes, there are problems in addition to losing money. First, when the pyramid collapses, any recruits you brought in will probably look to you to recoup their money. Second, there's the chance that you could go from victim to con artist without even realizing it. There are consumer protection statutes and criminal statutes with regard to pyramid schemes. Whether you're an unsuspecting victim or a full-fledged con artist, if you're violating those laws by recruiting new members, you're subject to prosecution. Although prosecutors typically don't prosecute the victims, it is a possibility that a fine or some other minimal sentence could be imposed.

Protecting Yourself From Pyramid Schemes

Research any promoter and investment you're considering:

- Ask if the investment is registered. Pyramids are illegal and can't register with any federal or state agency. If it's not registered, ask why.
- Check with the state securities commissioner, the Better Business Bureau, and the local district attorney to find out if the company and the promoter are legitimate.
- Be wary of promises of quick, substantial profits that require little work and effort on your part. Be sure the company has some substance from an economic point of view, such as legitimate products that could stand on their own.
- Don't buy in to a company that tells you that in addition to selling a product, you have to recruit other people to be distributors.
- If there are products to sell, find out if there's a market for them, if the company helps with advertising and distribution, and if the company has a buyback policy for unsold inventory. Check to see if the products are really being sold, determine their value versus their price, and identify the source of supply.
- Get copies of the company's marketing plan, sales literature, and other documentation. Be sure these materials are clear,

understandable, and sensible. If you're not sure, have a
trusted adviser read them.

- Don't buy in because a friend is trying to recruit you. Remember that in a pyramid scheme, for one person to make
  money, someone else has to lose money. If you're the newest
  recruit, that person losing money is you.

Knowing how to identify a Ponzi or pyramid scheme may
be the only safeguard you have from falling victim.

Janet Mortenson, Attorney, Houston, Texas

Anyone can be taken in by a Ponzi scheme. We had a case in
Texas in which a mortgage company made mobile home loans,
packaged the loans, and then sold them to investors. They
promised high rates of return and said the investment was
backed by the full faith and credit of the U.S. government, which
wasn't true. They printed documents that looked legitimate and
their story sounded plausible—so plausible, in fact, that even a
major airline invested $1.4 million with them.

It was a classic Ponzi scheme in which they were paying off early
investors with money collected from later investors. What made
it so difficult to figure out was that the company itself was legitimately authorized to participate in some government-backed
programs. But rather than selling investors the securities that
were backed by the programs in which it was authorized to participate, they sold bogus loan packages.

When a prospective investor called the Department of Housing
and Urban Development or the Government National Mortgage
Association to check out the company and the investment, if the
person didn't ask exactly the right questions, which was likely,
he or she would get an assurance that made it sound as though
the investment was legitimate. It was very complex.

The company was able to raise seventeen million dollars in a
short amount of time. In the end, the victims got back only a
few cents on the dollar.

This scam proves that you can't be too careful. You always have
to be skeptical. If there's even one small issue that makes you feel

uncomfortable, trust your instincts. It could save you from making a costly mistake.

Checklist

Is the person:

❑   Offering you huge returns in a can't-lose money-making scheme?

❑   Offering you an investment in a company whose business plan is impossible to understand?

❑   Promoting the investment only through word of mouth?

❑   Encouraging investors to reinvest their profits?

❑   Encouraging you to recruit other salespeople into the organization rather than assisting you in selling a product?

❑   Giving you substandard products to sell for high prices?

❑   Claiming you can earn big profits without doing much work?

If you answered yes to any of these questions, you may be looking at a Ponzi or pyramid scheme.

CHAPTER 6

High Tech—High Cost

Discourse on virtue and they pass by in droves; whistle and dance the shimmy and you've got an audience!

DIOGENES OF SINOPE, PHILOSOPHER

D id you hear the one about the time machine? There's this guy who says he's starting a new high-tech company. In order to get it off the ground, he needs money, so he starts selling stock in the company. The name of the company is Time Machines, Inc., of the United Kingdom. He says the product this company is going to produce is a super-high-tech time machine that can travel forward and backward in time. He doesn't quite have the technology he needs yet to make the time machine work, so he tells his potential investors that he's going to get that technology in one of two ways: (1) He's going to develop it or (2) he's going to create a Web site that's so sophisticated and so high tech that it will become so well known that someone in the future will see it, travel back in time, and give him the technology he needs for the time machine.

Pretty funny, huh? In fact, it's not funny at all, because it's not a joke. This is an actual fraud that a con artist perpetrated over the Internet. The story is a great testimonial as to just how convincing these con artists can be.

People often believe that any investment that is high tech has to be successful. Considering how some of the new high-tech companies of the near past have performed, why shouldn't they think that? Look at Microsoft Corporation. An investor who bought one hundred shares of Microsoft Corporation stock at $21 per share in the company's initial public offering on March 13, 1986, would have made an investment of $2,100. Approximately twelve and a half years later, after seven stock splits, that investment would be worth about $908,800 at its then current price of $142 per share.

Look at Cisco Systems. A purchase of one hundred shares at its February 16, 1990, initial public offering price of $18 per share would have represented an investment of $1,800. After seven stock splits in almost nine years, that investment would be worth $694,800 at its then current price of $96.50 per share.

And look at Dell Computer Corporation. A purchase of one hundred shares at its June 22, 1988, initial public offering price of $8.50 per share would represent an investment of $850. After six splits in ten and a half years, that investment would be worth $360,000 at its then current price of approximately $75 per share.

And we can't forget eBay, Inc., which went public on September 23, 1998, at a per share price of $18. A purchase of one hundred shares would have cost $1,800. eBay's shares skyrocketed to $311.25 per share, making that $1,800 investment worth $31,125 in less than three months!

Because those are astronomical gains, we hear about them on radio and television news and read about them in newspapers and magazines all the time. When we hear about this level of success, we want to get in on it. But what we don't hear about is that for every Microsoft, Cisco Systems, Dell Computer, and eBay, Inc., there are dozens of other high-tech companies that have gone out of business or generated practically no returns to their investors. The term *high tech* is not synonymous with success. Because a company is located in the Silicon Valley doesn't guarantee its stock price will soar. Just like any other type of company in any other industry, a high-tech investment has to be investigated to determine its merits and pitfalls.

Investigating this industry can be difficult because it's always in a state of flux. For instance, if an investor wants to get involved in the purchasing and leasing of planes, he can research the industry and learn about the types of planes that lessors prefer, learn how the deals work, and understand the positives and negatives of the investment. With a high-tech investment, by the time the investor starts researching and learning what the products are and how they work, they're obsolete; the industry has moved on to the product's next generation. With a technology-related product, no one can tell the general investment public what to look for and what questions to ask, because the industry changes too quickly.

Another reason that high-tech investments are dangerous is that most investors don't understand the new technologies well enough to know if what they're being told is accurate. If you invest in a real estate development deal that's fraudulent, some of the excuses you might hear from the con artist when the development isn't progressing as promised are that there was a problem with the title to the land, the builder ran into problems and won't be able to start building for another six weeks, or weather problems created delays. You can understand these excuses, do a little checking, and make an educated determination as to whether they're valid.

In a high-tech investment, the first problem is that you may not have a complete grasp of the industry or product. Then the excuses you receive as to why an investment isn't producing may be so complicated and use such confusing terminology that you have no idea whether they're valid. With the integration of cable, telephone, computers, and the Internet, plus terminology and concepts such as *digital certifications, cybercash,* and *electronic money,* con artists can create a thick cloud of confusion. If you don't understand, it's impossible to know whether you should be skeptical. The con artist, on the other hand, doesn't necessarily have to worry about the facts. He just has to be sure he's convincing.

The Wireless Cable Services Scam

The onslaught of high-tech scams began in the 1980s when wireless cable services were developed. The scamsters developed a three-phase scam.

Phase One

The first phase is the lottery scam. In the 1980s the Federal Communications Commission (FCC) began issuing licenses for certain new products. The first was wireless cable, for which a person could purchase the license to supply wireless cable services to a specific area. The licenses for the major cities, the primary markets, were sold to the highest bidders, and the second- and third-tier markets were auctioned off in a lottery. There were tens of thousands of applicants for a fairly small number of licenses available for auction.

Con artists have a tendency to follow the headlines. Whatever the hot investment is in the real world, the con artists dream up a scam in which they make their investment look like the real thing, but in reality it is a fraud. News of these lotteries was in the headlines at that time, so most people were familiar with the concept. That made the lotteries the perfect vehicle for a scam.

The con artist's pitch in this phase is that if you give him five thousand dollars, he'll put you in the FCC lottery. He guarantees you'll be successful because, he says, he knows how to file the lottery application and how to deal with the strict technical requirements. Once the license is purchased, the con artist will manage it for you. You just have to sit back and collect the money from this valuable license. Or he may say you can be one of many investors in a partnership or limited liability corporation that he's formed to purchase the licenses.

Because people had read about the FCC lotteries and wireless cable technology, they knew that the technology and the plan to sell them existed, so the pitch sounded plausible. In many cases, however, the con artist never even submitted an application for the investor. Instead, he took the money and ran. In other cases, he may have actually submitted the application but charged the investor far more than what the application process actually cost and pocketed the difference. If a license was acquired, the investor usually hadn't been told that an FCC license is only permission to use the airwaves to provide communication services. The owner still has to develop a communications system in compliance with FCC rules. That can be complicated and expensive. The con artist may also tell the investor that he can buy a license, then resell it or lease it to a communications company. But that market doesn't really exist, because those companies buy the licenses at inception rather than dealing with a third party; and, in fact, selling or leasing a license may even violate FCC rules.

Phase Two

In 1992, American Microtel, a Las Vegas company, was fraudulently offering investors wireless cable lottery services. Several states worked together and took enforcement action against the company to stop it from pursuing these activities. American Microtel then began claiming to potential investors that it owned the wireless cable license for a specific location and was putting together a group of investors to invest in the actual building and start-up of the wireless cable operation and business.

The build-out is the second phase of this scam. Just as American Microtel claimed, the pitch is that the company contacting you already owns a valuable license for a specific area and is ready to do a build-out of the wireless cable service. In order to do that, it needs to raise several million dollars to build a transmission tower and sign up subscribers. Therefore, it is forming a partnership or limited liability company in which you can invest. The con man tells you that the value of the license is based on the number of television sets located in the area the license covers, multiplied by some arbitrary number that is supposed to represent the income per television set. The value determined typically is in the tens of millions of dollars.

The problems are many. These people may not own the license. If they do own it, they're probably misrepresenting the value of it or they have no intention or technical ability to do a build-out. Once again, your money is gone.

Phase Three

Phase three is the recovery room scam. You get a call from some very sympathetic person who feels terrible that those awful people stole your money in a lottery scam and a build-out scam. If you give this person five thousand dollars, he'll either get your money back for you or turn your bad investment into a good investment by taking over the company and making it work. You guessed it: bye-bye money.

Scams With New Technology

As other high-tech products were developed, the con artists created new scams by applying these three phases to the new technology. When the FCC started lotteries to award licenses for interactive video data services, the scamsters took it through all three phases. When the FCC began issuing specialized mobile radio licenses, the con artists took it through all three phases. When the FCC started lotteries to award licenses for paging services, phase one, phase two, and phase three started all over again with that technology. The authorities see wave after wave of scams using these three phases as each new technology hits the marketplace.

Con artists have also created other scams that focus on high-tech products. For instance, you may have received a call from someone wanting to set up a 900 phone number for you. The number can be for a psychic service or a dating service or anything else you want. You pay twenty-five thousand dollars and he'll handle the very technical work of obtaining the 900 number and setting it all up. You'll then collect a certain amount of money from each call received.

In this scam, the con artist does indeed set up the 900 number for you. You can call it yourself and check it out. Part of the problem is that you paid twenty-five thousand dollars for something that in reality probably cost about five hundred dollars (to get the number from the phone company and set it up). It's an easy process and takes very little technical expertise. The other part of the problem is that you're told you'll collect a certain amount of money from each call. But what if there aren't any calls?

In order to call the 900 number, people need to know it exists. The only way they can know it exists is if it's advertised on TV or radio, in magazines or newspapers. The con artist, however, has not mentioned anything about marketing, because he isn't planning on doing any. So you sit there for three months waiting for the money to start rolling in. By the time you realize there's a problem, the con artist's phone line has been disconnected and you can't find him to complain.

High-tech scams are marketed in several ways. The Internet has opened a new frontier of high-tech investment scams. Telemarketers love high-tech scams. Stock investment frauds thrive on supposed high-tech companies. But no matter what type of high-tech investment the con artists are pushing or which delivery vehicle they use, the problem is always the same: The investment involves misrepresentation and fraud with respect to the value of the service being provided and the return you can expect from the product, and there is also a question as to whether the product exists at all.

Protecting Yourself From High-Tech Scams

High-tech companies and investments can be complicated and confusing. Often when investors don't understand something, they think it's because they're stupid. But the truth is that they don't understand something because it doesn't make any sense. Con artists are never impeded by the truth; they'll tell you anything to get you to invest, whether it's sensible or not. You'll be told you're getting in on the ground floor of the next Microsoft, IBM, or Intel.

It's hard to separate fact from fiction because some of the innovations we're seeing today that are actually legitimate seem so impossible that you'd think they're fiction. At the same time, the con artists use those innovations we're reading about to perpetrate fraud. The biggest single factor as to why high-tech fraud works so well is its complexity and the ease of confusing people.

If you decide to invest in a high-tech investment, follow all the rules of investigating any type of investment. In addition, if the offer is to purchase a license in an auction for you, find out the following information:

- Has the FCC actually scheduled an auction, as the company claims?
- Will the type of service the license is supposed to represent be included in that auction?
- Is the company that's making the offer registered with the FCC to be a bidder in the auction?
- Obtain a copy of the company's audited financial statements and determine whether the company is prosperous enough to afford the license and the build-out.
- If the license is to be purchased from a private source, call the

    FCC and ask the original cost of the license and who pur-
chased it.

- Inquire as to whether there have been enhancements that
  would make the license more valuable than its original purchase price.
- Ask the promoter how much of your investment will go
  toward commissions and fees.

    Always be careful of promoters who want you to invest in
high-tech-related partnerships or limited liability corporations in
which you have to invest at least twenty-five thousand dollars. And
never believe the claim that an investment has been approved by
the government for an Individual Retirement Account (IRA). The
government gives no such approvals for any investments.

    High-tech fraud is a constantly moving target. New break-
throughs in technology mean new types of frauds. The authorities
have no idea how much high-tech fraud is perpetrated each year,
primarily because most of it is never reported. Dick Johnston, director of the National White Collar Crime Center in Richmond, Virginia, likens it to the crimes of domestic violence and rape prior to
the 1970s. Everyone knew they existed and were horrible. But there
wasn't much that could be done; no one was advocating for remedies, there were no strong laws on the books pertaining to these
crimes, and you couldn't expect good results if you did go to the
authorities. Victims felt embarrassed and ashamed. So the crimes
went unreported.

    High-tech fraud is at that stage today. It's difficult to prose-
cute, you probably won't get good results if you do report it, and
victims are embarrassed and ashamed that they allowed themselves
to be defrauded. So it goes unreported, and the con artists continue to work their cons, which can be very large.

    As with any other type of investment, you are your own
best line of defense. If the investment doesn't make sense to you,
there's probably something wrong. Check out the salesperson and
firm, ask a trusted adviser for help, and don't jump into an investment you don't understand. Common sense and that gnawing
feeling in your stomach may be telling you something. Be sure to
listen.

Bill McDonald, Enforcement Director, California Department of Corporations (the state securities regulator for California)

Con artists use high-tech investment scams in any way they can. We've even seen pension administrators put their IRA customers into high-tech deals that were total scams. In 1994, the regulators in California subpoenaed the records of a pension administrator, Qualified Pensions, Inc., and found that they had put their IRA customers into 141 wireless cable and other high-tech deals—not a conservative IRA investment. In September 1995, the SEC obtained an injunction against the company for misappropriation of IRA funds and unlicensed broker-dealer activity.

Money invested in an IRA is expected to generate steady returns for several years, so that's how the con artists tried to sell these high-tech investments. They told their victims that wireless cable was cutting-edge technology; the truth was that by the time the victims put their money in this investment, the technology had already become obsolete due to the introduction of satellites. But the con artists were making projections as to the number of wireless cable towers that would be built twenty years out. They were making twenty-year earnings projections, when in reality the technology was obsolete before the investment was even made.

In 1994 in California, we stopped one hundred scams and charged 426 people with illegal investments valued at over $850 million. These investments were scams from the beginning. But the FCC practically aided and abetted the con artists from the standpoint that they knew these lotteries were being used as vehicles for scams and they never got the word out or tightened up on the lotteries. The FCC still hasn't done anything about the fact that their products are being used to scam people and have been for years. In fact, they're still making product available.

Investors have to do their own research on these investments, and that can be difficult. The best rule to follow is that if you can't verify the value and the existence of an investment, don't invest.

Checklist

Is the person:

❑ Claiming that an investment will reap huge profits simply because it's high tech?

❑ Offering an investment that's too technical to understand?

❑ Answering your questions with technical jargon you don't understand?

❑ Offering to file an FCC license lottery application for you and promising to resell the license?

❑ Claiming to own an FCC license and wanting you to invest for the build-out phase?

❑ Offering, for a fee, to recover your money from a previous FCC license scam?

❑ Offering to set up a 900 phone number for you, but not mentioning the marketing aspects of the number?

❑ Claiming an investment has been approved by the government for IRAs?

If you answered yes to any of these questions, you're dealing with a high-tech scam con artist.

PART FOUR

SCAMS ON WALL STREET

CHAPTER 7

Tricks of the Trade: The Unscrupulous Stockbroker

Assumption is the mother of all screw-ups.

WETHERN'S LAW

If you invest with someone you don't know who calls you on the phone, you're making a big mistake. You need to find a stockbroker, check her out, be sure she's someone you feel comfortable with and you trust, and then develop a long-term relationship. Unfortunately, even then you can't be sure.

Michael John Sullo entered the investment business in the late 1980s by opening the M. John Sullo Financial Group in Connecticut. Money problems began to plague him after he started managing a nightclub. To keep the club afloat, he needed money, so he started funneling his clients' investments into it. He targeted his more inexperienced clients and withheld official documents about the investments. He also convinced clients to turn over power of attorney to him.

Seventeen investors in Connecticut had been doing business with Sullo from 1990 to 1993. During those three years he promised his clients high returns. Instead, he stole $930,619 from them. His seventeen clients lost retirement nest eggs, homes, and a lifetime of savings.

Sullo used the money he collected from his clients to pay

expensive restaurant tabs, make lease payments for his nightclub, pay for his son's college tuition, and support his own lifestyle. The April 6, 1995, issue of the *New Haven Register* ran an article on Sullo with the tag line "Evil human being sentenced in Milford." Because of some of the tactics Sullo employed, many believed that characterization was accurate. For instance, according to his own affidavit, Sullo had one client who finally told him she had no more money to invest. Rather than leave her alone, he drove her to the bank and instructed her to take a cash advance of twenty thousand dollars on her credit cards.

When Sullo was arrested, he was broke. He pleaded guilty to sixteen counts of first-degree larceny and twenty counts of fraudulent sales of securities. He was sent to prison for ten years plus five years of probation. Upon his release, he's ordered to pay 15 percent of his income or two hundred dollars per month—whichever is greater—until he reimburses his victims. At two hundred dollars per month, that'll take about 387 years.

Typically if a stockbroker is a con artist, you'll encounter problems fairly quickly. Maybe the first two or three trades he makes for your account will be in line with your investment goals and risk tolerance. Then, on the fourth trade he may stray from your investment objectives and try to talk you into an investment that differs from those he typically suggests. Before you know it, you're trading in high-risk stocks that the firm is selling from its own inventory or investments that earn the broker higher commissions. Or the broker could be putting your money in investments that the brokerage firm isn't even aware of. These types of problems usually occur within the first twelve to eighteen months of the broker-client relationship.

But just because you've been working with a stockbroker for five years and never encountered a problem doesn't mean one can't develop. Stockbrokers are human beings with the same problems that other human beings encounter. Your broker may end up in an expensive divorce or may become addicted to drugs or gambling. Or maybe the market takes a downturn and his clients are afraid to make trades or to put more money into the market, so his commissions decrease. When his revenue stream drops, he still has car payments and mortgage payments to make and groceries to buy. That's when he may begin thinking about increasing his income through inappropriate conduct.

There are four types of illegal acts that stockbrokers typically use to enhance their income at their clients' expense: unauthorized trades, churning, unsuitability, and theft.

Unauthorized Trades

An unauthorized trade is one in which the stockbroker buys or sells a security without the client's permission. Suddenly a stock you never heard of appears on your monthly statement. When you call, the broker says he thought it would be a good stock for you. Or he may remind you that you were on vacation and he couldn't check with you, or some other excuse. If regulators become involved, the broker says he was acting on oral instructions from you. Since it's the broker's word against yours, prosecution is difficult. And often prosecution isn't even pursued because the brokerage firm will quickly reverse the unauthorized trade to avoid having to deal with authorities.

One investor who had an unauthorized trade problem, however, was able to prove he hadn't given his broker oral instructions. The customer, a pilot for Delta Airlines, alleged three unauthorized trades. When regulators investigated, they found that the trades were time-stamped at 2:54 P.M. and 2:55 P.M. eastern time. The pilot's log showed that he had landed at 3:19 P.M. in Atlanta that day after a transatlantic flight from Germany. The regulators readily agreed that pilots typically don't talk to their brokers when they're on final approach.

Unfortunately, most people don't have the ability to prove they didn't give their broker permission for trades. Therefore, if it happens, stop it immediately. Never allow a broker to get away with doing an unauthorized trade in your account because once he starts, it gets easier and easier. As soon as you let one unauthorized trade pass, it will be a downhill slope from there.

Churning

Stockbrokers are in business for one thing: to earn commissions. The more securities they buy and sell for clients, the more commissions they earn. Your stockbroker may recommend that you buy a stock, then a couple weeks later encourage you to sell it because it's up a point and he doesn't think it'll go any higher, or because it's down a point and you need to get out before it goes down further. On the next recommended stock purchase, he also encourages you to sell earlier than what he originally suggested. Before long, you're trading weekly, generating plenty of commissions for the broker. Sometimes these trades are made without the customer's knowledge, as was the case with an elderly man with mental and physical disabilities who was confined to a nursing home. Without his knowledge, his broker churned his account, generating $24,000 in commissions on a $343,000 account. In other cases, customers will agree to this type of short-term trading based on their broker's advice, not realizing the amount of money it's costing them until it's too late.

To determine if your broker is churning your account, look at the motive and the story he gives you for suggesting trades. Let's say your broker suggests you buy ABC Corporation at seventy-five dollars per share because he thinks it's going to ninety-five dollars per share soon. If the stock goes to ninety-five dollars and he suggests you sell it, the reason he gives for selling the stock matches the story he gave you originally. Now let's say that he suggests that you buy ABC Corporation at seventy-five dollars per share because your investment objective is income and ABC Corporation pays a dividend yielding 5 percent. If the stock goes up three points and he suggests you sell it, his reason for selling doesn't match his story for buying. Remember that the reason for the purchase was to collect the dividend income. If that dividend is secure, why would you sell the stock? One possible reason may be that the broker is trying to churn your account. Also, if the commissions you pay for buying and selling a stock are more than the gains you make, the broker is making more money than you are. Look at the trades your broker suggests and the amount of time the stocks are held, and determine who's profiting.

Another way to determine churning is by turnover. If you have twenty thousand dollars in stocks and you sell all twenty thousand dollars' worth and buy twenty thousand dollars' worth of other stocks in the same year, you've turned your portfolio 100 percent. If your broker suggests so much trading that your portfolio is turning one full time in a year, you should definitely question his motives and determine who's making more profit: you or the broker.

Unsuitability

Unsuitability means that the broker is selling you investments that are not suitable in meeting the investment objectives you've outlined. For instance, if you're retired and your investment objectives are current income consistent with safety of principal, and the broker puts you in stocks that pay little or no dividends, those investments are unsuitable. Or maybe you have a twelve-year-old and a fourteen-year-old and you list your investment objective as wanting to save for their college education. If the broker puts you in securities that have no growth potential, that's unsuitable. It's almost always unsuitable if a broker convinces a client who wants safety of principal to trade on margin (borrowing money to buy additional securities).

If your broker recommends a new type of investment that's different from the typical securities you purchase, ask why. The reason may be that he earns a higher commission for that investment versus another that might be a better fit for you. Or the firm may be offering sales incentives or sponsoring a sales contest in which the broker who sells the most of that particular investment wins a trip to Hawaii.

Theft

Maybe your broker needs a sizable chunk of money quickly and sees twenty thousand dollars' worth of a specific stock in your portfolio. He may sell the stock without notifying you and then pocket the money. Of course, on your next monthly statement, you'll see that twenty thousand dollars' worth of stock is missing from your portfolio—right? Maybe not. Ralph Lambiase, securities director for the state of Connecticut, says he's seen cases where computer-literate brokers print out a monthly statement that shows the stock is still in the account. If you receive a statement that is clearly different from the firm's typical statement, call the branch manager—not the broker—and ask if the firm has changed its statement.

Another way a broker can benefit at your expense is by *sell-*

ing away—making trades of investment products that don't go through the brokerage house he's licensed with. Because the firm does not endorse these investment products (and probably doesn't even know the broker is selling them), it can't research the investment to determine whether it's one they want to sell. For instance, your broker may convince you to invest fifty thousand dollars for a part interest in his brother's new restaurant. You sell stock out of your account, and the fifty thousand dollars leaves the brokerage firm. A year later when the restaurant goes bankrupt, you complain to the brokerage firm. But the firm isn't even aware of this investment and will probably say it's not its problem. It may fire the broker, but your loss is your loss. There are, of course, some firms that don't want their reputation to be tarnished, so they may help you out. Otherwise, your only recourse may be a civil lawsuit against the broker and the brokerage firm challenging the firm's supervisory procedures over the broker.

Protecting Yourself From Unscrupulous Stockbrokers

It's up to you to monitor your brokerage account and review your stockbroker's performance. No broker will ever call you and say, "I wanted you to know that the Dow went up 17 percent this year. Your account, however, went up only 5 percent. In the meantime, I've earned a lot of commissions off your account." It's also up to you to check the trade confirmation slips you receive after each trade. If there's a problem, such as the dollar amount of the trade agreed upon is incorrect, call the broker and follow up that call with a letter outlining your conversation. Then make sure you receive a corrected confirmation slip. Also check your monthly account statements for questionable activity. Let's say that one month you notice that you have two hundred shares of a specific stock in your account, but last month you had five hundred shares and you didn't authorize a sale. So you call the broker, and he says he'll correct it on your next statement. When you get your next statement, it's still wrong. You call and complain, and he apologizes and promises it'll be right on the next statement.

Later, when the regulators start investigating this stockbroker, they're going to look at your account and say this problem existed for two months, and during that time you received a confirmation slip and two monthly statements, and you never sent in a complaint. Because there's no record, the regulator assumes the sale of the three hundred shares was done with your consent.

When you see incorrect information on your trade confirmation slips or monthly statement, complain immediately in writing. Even if you call the stockbroker and he says he'll correct it, follow up that call with a letter reiterating the problem and confirming that the stockbroker said he'll resolve it.

It's also important that you submit your investment objectives to your stockbroker in writing. If that information is documented, the broker can't change it on you. If he later recommends a stock to you that doesn't fit your investment objectives, ask plenty of questions.

Let's say your broker knows that your investment objectives are safety of principal with income. You get a call from him suggesting you buy one hundred shares of Con Men Computer Company. Should you do it? Before you can answer that question, there are a few questions you need to ask and a little research you should do:

- *"Why do you think this is a good investment for me?"* If he's recommending it to you, he must think it fits your investment criteria. Find out why. Ask him how this particular stock will mesh with your objectives for your portfolio.
- *"What kind of company is it?"* The name says it's a computer company, but does it make computers, computer chips, computer software, or boxes that computers are shipped in? The answer makes a big difference. While the computer chip industry may be the fastest-growing industry around, the software industry may be a laggard. This company may not meet your investment objective of safety.
- *"What is the stock's price?"* If the stock sells for one hundred dollars per share, buying one hundred shares may make it such a large investment that it represents too large a percentage of your portfolio. If it sells for under five dollars a share, that may be indicative of a stock that's too risky for your needs.
- *"What is the company's financial track record?"* Have revenues and earnings been increasing, decreasing, or been volatile or

stagnant for the past five or ten years? Are expenses and debt increasing disproportionately to the increases in sales?

- *"What is the company's price-to-earnings ratio?"* If it's trading for a higher-than-normal price-to-earnings ratio (price per share divided by earnings per share) based on the stock's history and the company's competitors, what warrants the high price? If it's overpriced, it doesn't fit the objective of safety.

- *"How long has the company been in business, and how stiff is the competition?"* If this is a start-up company with no track record, this stock doesn't represent safety. If it's an established company that has been in business for years, find out what percentage of the market it holds, its prospects for gaining market share through new products or cost savings, and if new competition is on the horizon.

- *"What are the risks?"* If this recommendation isn't the typical type of security you usually buy, ask why he's recommending something different. Find out what types of risks and fees are associated with the investment.

- *"Can you send me research reports and company documents?"* Just because the stockbroker tells you about a security doesn't mean you don't need to check it out. Get the prospectus, annual report, quarterly reports, 10-K, 10-Qs, proxies, and other research reports and read through them. Check out the company's Web site. Take time to understand the investment, and be sure it's being sold to you for the right reasons. There are plenty of risks in the stock market: inflation risk, interest rate risk, market risk, and in some cases currency and political risk. Why add the risk of being defrauded by an unscrupulous stockbroker? Take the time to understand the investment.

- *"Where will I get the money for this investment?"* Is the broker suggesting that you take money from a savings account or that you sell your IBM stock to purchase a fairly risky stock? Consider whether it makes sense to trade one investment for the other.

If your stockbroker doesn't give satisfactory answers to your questions, don't buy the stock. Tell the broker you don't think the investment is right for you, and leave it at that. Don't be bullied into buying something you're not comfortable with. It's the broker's job to help you meet your investment objectives, sometimes by recommending a purchase, sometimes by recommending a sale, and sometimes by recommending restraint. Your role is to make the decisions and take responsibility for protecting your assets. Regulators, law enforcement personnel, and the courts don't have the resources required to protect us from those who want to steal our money. Each of us must accept that responsibility for ourselves.

Ralph Lambiase, Securities Director, Department of Banking, State of Connecticut

A lot of the stockbrokers who end up defrauding their customers didn't start out with that type of activity in mind. But sometimes they get into financial trouble and become desperate. The easiest way for them to get quick cash is to steal it from their customers.

Only a small percentage of stockbrokers engage in illicit conduct, including defrauding their customers. But consider that there are about 5,600 brokerage firms and about 560,000 people who are registered to sell securities. If just 3 or 4 percent of those people are unethical, you're talking significant numbers. Plus, each broker has maybe one hundred or two hundred accounts. Look at how many people can be affected!

The public thinks that we, as regulators, are at the branches conducting regular examinations, but there are sixty thousand branches, and the state securities regulators have the capacity to look at one thousand of them a year at most. To make matters worse, we used to require the branches to maintain a minimum number of books and records on-site at the branch office. But the National Securities Market Improvement Act in 1996 said the states can no longer require the branches to keep records that the SEC doesn't require. So now when we do conduct examinations, we don't even have access to the books and records we need. The SEC is considering new rules that may address this problem. For the most part, unless someone complains about a stockbroker's committing a fraudulent act, we're not going to hear about it.

The public really has to protect itself. If a stockbroker recommends a stock that you don't know and he can't explain why you should buy it, don't buy it. Why let yourself be hustled by a guy you're paying? Take control, monitor your monthly statements, and make your own decisions. If you don't, by the time you realize a problem has developed, it's probably too late. Your money is already gone.

Checklist

Is the stockbroker:

- ❑ Making trades that aren't in line with your stated investment objectives and risk tolerance level?
- ❑ Making trades you never authorized?
- ❑ Suggesting sell trades that aren't in line with the original reason for buying that stock?
- ❑ Profiting more from your trading activity than you are?
- ❑ Recommending so many trades that your total portfolio turns one full time in a year?
- ❑ Suggesting that you trade on margin when your investment objective is safety of principal?
- ❑ Recommending a new type of investment that's different from the securities you typically purchase?
- ❑ Sending you a monthly brokerage statement that is clearly different from the firm's usual statement?
- ❑ Offering you investments that are not endorsed by the brokerage firm for which the stockbroker works?
- ❑ Sending you incorrect trade confirmation slips and not immediately correcting the error when you complain?
- ❑ Giving you unsatisfactory or vague answers to your questions?

If you answered yes to these questions, you may be dealing with an unscrupulous stockbroker.

CHAPTER 8

Micro-Cap Stocks Don't Generate Micro Losses

*A lie gets halfway around the world before the truth
has a chance to get its pants on.*

SIR WINSTON CHURCHILL, BRITISH STATESMAN AND PRIME MINISTER

From July 1997 to February 1998, more than 150 investors received calls offering them the opportunity to invest in a five-million-dollar private offering for a company called ConnecTechnologies. ConnecTechnologies, these investors were told, was a company that would prosper by solving the year 2000 computer problem. The promise was that shortly after investors invested in the private offering, the company would go public through an initial public offering (IPO). Investors would then make a lot of money as the company's stock price increased on the open market.

Many of these calls to investors were made by Adam Stone, a senior account executive with Stone Asset, Inc., who said his offices were located in the World Trade Center in New York City. Investors poured nine hundred thousand dollars into this investment, only to learn later that several pieces of information they had been given weren't quite accurate:

- Adam Stone didn't exist. Adam Stone was a fictitious house name that Stone Asset encouraged its sales agents to use.

- Stone Asset was located in the World Trade Center, as the sales agents stated, but it wasn't there legally. The employees gained access to the building by fraudulently obtaining building passes under a corporate name other than Stone Asset.
- The sales agents were not registered with the State of New York, nor was the firm.
- The statements the sales agents made to potential investors about the prosperous future of ConnecTechnologies were misleading or outright false. In reality, ConnecTechnologies conducted no business and had no revenues or profits. Hence there could be no initial public offering.
- Of the nine hundred thousand dollars that investors put into the investment, six hundred thousand dollars was funneled back to the principals and employees of Stone Asset.

The good news is that the New York attorney general's office closed down Stone Asset and charged the principals with securities fraud, failure to register, and persistent and repeated fraud and illegal activities arising from the solicitation and sale of securities. The people who operated Stone Asset are the type of con artists investors face when they're scammed in a micro-cap stock fraud.

Micro-cap stocks are stocks of small companies, usually start-ups, that are very risky, typically generate no revenues, and have no short-term prospects of generating any revenues. They are defined as companies having less than three hundred million dollars in capitalization, but many have no capitalization at all. Typically only one brokerage firm, the one that brings the company public, trades the stock.

Micro-cap stocks are a legitimate and important part of our economy. Without the ability to raise money by selling stock, many small companies would never obtain the financing they need to remain in business. And there are plenty of success stories of micro-cap stocks that do well and make money for both the company and its investors. The problem is that because they trade at very low prices, micro-cap stocks can be easily manipulated, making them ripe for fraud.

The Background

Micro-cap stock fraud has its roots in the scams that used to be per-petrated with penny stocks—those that sell for less than five dollars per share. Scams involving these stocks started in the 1940s in the West, where investors were sold worthless shares of gold- and silver-mining companies. Penny stock fraud was confined to the western states until the 1970s, when it started to take root in the East. According to the New York State attorney general's 1997 *Report on Micro-Cap Stock Fraud*, in 1985 there were only 55 penny stock firms in the country, all of them in five states. By 1990, there were approximately 325 of these firms with main offices in more than twenty-five states, operating thousands of branches through-out the country.

The SEC curtailed penny stock scams in 1990 by enacting tougher restrictions on penny stock promoters. The law now requires brokers to provide extensive written information and make certain disclosures about a stock if it sells for less than five dollars per share. Brokers can no longer sell penny stocks by making cold calls, and they have to be concerned about suitability—that is, ensuring that an investment is right for a specific investor.

Birth of a Scam

When penny stock fraud dried up, micro-cap stock fraud was born. In order to get around the penny stock rules, the con artists con-tinue to run the same scams, but use stocks that sell for just over five dollars per share, sidestepping the definition of penny stocks. Or they often combine one or two shares of stock with one or two warrants and call the package a "unit" in order to create a security with a composite price of more than five dollars. (A warrant is an option to buy stock in the future at a specified price.)

The SEC rules state that brokers can't sell a micro-cap stock to a customer who has just opened an account, but they can sell micro-cap stocks to existing customers. To get around that rule, the con artist convinces an investor to open an account and buy a blue-chip stock, such as IBM or General Electric. After a week, if the blue-chip stock goes up in price, the con artist boasts that he put the investor in a stock that made money. He then encourages him to sell the blue-chip stock and buy a stock that, he says, can make a lot of money—a micro-cap stock. If the blue-chip stock went down in price, the con artist says he doesn't feel good about that stock and encourages the investor to sell out and buy something else—a micro-cap stock. Because the investor purchased the blue-chip stock, he is now an existing customer and the broker can sell him a micro-cap stock.

Domination and control are the mainstays of micro-cap stock fraud. First, the con artists obtain a dominant position in the stock of a company that is bankrupt or that's just a corporate shell and has no operations or revenues whatsoever. Purchasing all of a company's stock doesn't take an inordinate amount of money; the stock is extremely cheap since the company has no product or service, or the product or service it produces is not valuable.

The con artist may also illegally acquire Rule 144 stock or Regulation S stock, which are both restricted stocks that can't be legally traded for one or two years. He can buy this stock at extremely low prices. The swindler ignores the restriction and trades the stock in his scam.

In yet other instances, the company the con artist uses for this swindle may be a legitimate company that wants to go public, but the big brokerage firms won't underwrite the IPO because the company is too small or doesn't have a proved performance track record. In those cases, the company typically becomes a target of the fraud and loses right along with the investors.

Once the con artist has possession of the stock, he touts it through cold calls, press releases, or the Internet by misrepresenting the investment. He'll say the company is on the verge of a breakthrough such as a cure for AIDS, or is close to closing a big business deal that will double the price of the stock, or has a product that's beginning to generate a great deal of interest in the marketplace. Often these con artists use high-tech companies because investors have seen small, high-tech companies make huge gains as soon as they hit the marketplace. Investors are told they need to get in on the ground floor because this stock could be the next Intel, IBM, or Microsoft. They create a huge demand for the stock that is totally unrelated to the company's asset value.

For instance, in early 1998, Abbey-Ashford Securities, a Florida-based registered broker-dealer, allowed unregistered broker-dealer J. P. Michaels Associates to operate from its New York offices to sell securities. Michaels sold approximately three hundred victims two million dollars' worth of stock in two companies: J. P. Michaels Equities Corp. and Psychic Cafe. To generate the type of demand needed to sell the securities, brokers told investors that the two companies would go public shortly and that their investments would generate a return in the range of 50 percent to 3,000 percent. The truth was that there was no market for the stock, and the securities were totally worthless. No action was ever taken to take the companies public.

The demand these brokers generate by their misrepresentations is totally unrelated to the true asset value of the company. But once that demand is generated, the only stock available for sale in the marketplace is the stock that's controlled by the insiders. The brokers tell the investors that they'll charge them no commissions to buy the stock. What the investors don't know is that the broker is significantly marking up the price of the stock. In some cases, the IPO never happens because the con artist takes the money and runs.

If there is an IPO, all the hype and the buying will force the price of the stock to climb. The insiders slowly sell their stock at higher and higher prices. When the stock is at the highest level the insiders believe it will reach, they dump the remainder of their shares, the stock price plummets, and the investors are left with worthless stock. The stock price may have started at $5.50 per share, run up to $20.00 per share, and then after the insiders dump their stock, it settles at $.50. The insiders make money; the investors lose. When the stock collapses, the brokers typically claim they were misled by the company whose stock they were selling. This scam is known as the *pump and dump*. The insiders pump up the price of the shares, then dump the stock.

The ironic part is that in many cases investors don't realize they've been swindled until the authorities contact them. They simply assume they made a risky investment and lost, one of the pitfalls of investing in the micro-cap stock market.

There are times when investors can make money in micro-cap stock fraud deals. As the brokerage firm touts the stock and the price rises, an investor who bought in early and sells after the stock moves up has made a profit. But that does not mean he or she will collect the profit. Promoters of micro-cap stock fraud are usually adamant that the person invest the profits into another micro-cap stock that the firm is controlling.

Of course, just because a stock sells for five or six dollars per share doesn't mean it's part of a pump-and-dump scam. There are plenty of legitimate micro-cap stocks that investors can trade. Typically, though, even legitimate micro-cap stocks are fairly risky, and people who invest in these stocks should be investing only risk capital and understand that there's a good chance they could lose their total investment. Investors should also be aware that micro-cap stocks, whether legitimate or fraudulent, aren't traded on exchanges; therefore, they're not listed in the newspaper stock tables. That makes it difficult for investors to monitor a micro-cap stock's price.

In the past several years, there have been numerous IPOs that have been really hot. They hit the market at a price in the teens and after their first or second day of trading have doubled or tripled in price. But not all IPOs are hot. Many start off cold and just get colder. Andrew Kandel, chief of the Investor Protection and Securities Bureau in the New York State attorney general's office, likens the micro-cap stock market at its best to gambling in Atlantic City. At its worse, when there is manipulation involved, he says it's like gambling at Rick's Café in the film *Casablanca*, where the odds are fixed against you. If the broker and the brokerage firm don't want you to make money, you won't.

Cracking Down

There's one other player in this scenario whose responsibility to investors is currently being questioned: the clearing firms—large brokerage houses that handle the administrative paperwork, such as processing trades, for other brokerage firms and providing their customers with confirmations, account statements, and other documentation. The services they provide are legitimate and certainly needed for the markets to operate. Because the clearing firms are typically large, well-established, well-known brokerage firms, the con artists use their names in sales pitches to give investors a sense of security. These clearing firms, however, have no supervisory authority over the firms they clear for, nor do they have any legal responsibilities to those firms' clients.

The question arises as to whether it's the clearing firms' responsibility to investigate the brokerage firms that hire them for clearing activities if those firms have numerous complaints lodged against them. Some industry experts believe they should be responsible. The clearing firms believe their obligation is to process the trades, not review, scrutinize, and investigate. That question is under debate.

Micro-cap stock fraud has become extremely prevalent in the United States, but states are trying to crack down on these promoters by using a number of strategies such as licensing, the review of securities offerings, and tougher enforcement actions. In fact, in May 1997, twenty state securities agencies filed thirty-six actions against fourteen micro-cap stock firms. That was the largest ever coordinated state enforcement initiative aimed at a particular market sector.

In May 1998, Justice Colleen McMahon of the New York State Supreme Court handed down the longest prison sentence in recent memory for micro-cap stock fraud. She sentenced Robert Laws, the owner of Concorde Capital Group, to up to twenty-four years in prison. Laws and one of his salesmen were accused of stealing nearly a half-million dollars from fifty-five investors through their micro-cap stock fraud activities. The salesman was sentenced to three to nine years, and three other firm stockbrokers were given lesser sentences.

Just a week prior, four officials at Monroe Parker Securities were also arrested and charged with securities fraud stemming from manipulation of the sale and solicitation of micro-cap securities.

Although the states are cracking down on con artists and are certainly willing to give them prison sentences, one of the problems is that when regulators close down a fraudulent firm and prosecute the principals, they don't have the resources required to prosecute all the brokers, so the brokers are often free to move on to other firms and continue their fraudulent ways.

Protecting Yourself From Micro-Cap Fraud

If you're a regular investor, chances are that at some point in your investing career, you'll be approached by someone wanting to sell you a micro-cap stock. If a stockbroker suggests you buy a stock that sells for around five dollars per share, ask plenty of questions as to why you should purchase it, how it fits your investment strategy, and how it can enhance your portfolio. Read research material you obtain from the company and from third parties to determine if the company is valid and sound and is one you'd want to own. Check out the broker and the brokerage firm making the offer.

If you buy a micro-cap stock, monitor your account closely. If the price increases and you sell, don't let the broker convince you to plow the money back into another micro-cap stock without first doing your homework.

If you find you've been defrauded, report it immediately to the Securities & Exchange Commission and your state securities regulators. Your chances of recovering your money will be slim, but if your complaint causes the firm and the broker to be investigated and go out of business, you will save others from falling prey.

Investing in the stock market carries an inherent amount of risk. If, however, investors do their homework, research the stocks they purchase, and deal with honest and trustworthy stockbrokers, the stock market can also offer a fair amount of return. Balancing risk with return is the path to being a good investor. Dealing with a stockbroker you don't know and buying stocks you can't research is the path to trouble.

Judy Sheridan, Victim of Micro-Cap Stock Fraud

I was working with a stockbroker I really liked, but she left the brokerage firm and my account was assigned to another broker. I worked with him a while, but I really wasn't pleased with him. He was always condescending and constantly made comments that really upset me. Just when I was planning to find a new stockbroker, this guy named John called me. He was very nice. He said he was really good at picking stocks, and he always made his customers 25 to 30 percent returns. He even claimed to have written a book. I decided to give him a try, so I transferred my account to him.

He immediately sold some of my stocks and bought others—mostly stocks in the range of four to twelve dollars. The first few months, my account balance went up. But then in one month I lost fifteen thousand dollars. I called him, and he said it would turn around. But my account kept decreasing every month, and he kept telling me to have patience—it would come back. After a while, he quit accepting my calls.

It got so bad I didn't even like to get my statements. I'd throw them unopened in a drawer. I couldn't deal with it. It was too painful. I finally decided to get rid of him, and a friend recommended a local stockbroker. I took my statements to him, and he told me I had been defrauded. The companies whose stocks I owned were thinly capitalized and had a history of losses. They had never made a profit. That wasn't how those stocks had been presented to me.

I got the name of a securities attorney and took my statements to him, and we filed a lawsuit against the broker and the brokerage firm. When the attorney did some research, he found that John didn't have a license to sell securities in my state, had flunked the securities dealer exam several times, and had a history of changing firms about every eighteen months. One of the firms where he had worked had settled a dispute with a client who charged John with churning his account. I didn't know any of that until we filed the lawsuit. I had never thought to check him out because I didn't realize this type of thing went on. I just took him at face value. In the end, the attorney estimated that I lost twenty thousand dollars. In the lawsuit I got eight thousand dollars back.

It makes me angry that these people play such games. They take advantage of people with their slick talking just so they can make money. It's the lowest of the low. I think he should have been sent to jail, but for all I know, he's probably at another firm doing this to someone else.

I now work with a local broker who has me in much more solid stocks like General Electric. My attorney recommended him to me. But before I transferred my account to him, I went in and met him face-to-face. I advise everyone to do that.

Checklist

Is the stockbroker:

❏   Recommending that you buy micro-cap stocks that sell for just over five dollars per share?

❏   Selling you micro-cap stocks in a newly opened account?

❏   Encouraging you to sell a blue-chip stock to purchase a micro-cap stock?

❏   Claiming that a company whose stock sells at five dollars per share is on the verge of a major breakthrough?

❏   Encouraging you to get in on the ground floor of a micro-cap stock that will be the next IBM?

❏   Insisting that any profits made on a micro-cap stock should be invested in another micro-cap stock?

❏   Refusing to take your calls?

❏   Changing jobs frequently?

If you answered yes to any of these questions, you may be the targeted victim of micro-cap stock fraud.

CHAPTER 9

As If It's Not Risky Enough, the Con Artists Had to Jump In: Commodity Fraud

I steal.

SAM GIANCANA, CHICAGO GANGSTER,
EXPLAINING HIS LIVELIHOOD TO HIS DRAFT BOARD

In the early 1980s, gold was selling for around eight hundred dollars an ounce, and a lot of people wanted to buy it as an investment because they thought it would continue to rise in price. But holding on to gold can be inconvenient. Whether it is held in the form of bars or coins, storage can create difficulties. Moreover, it can be stolen, so it has to be kept in a safe place, and it needs to be insured.

William and James Alderdice, who founded the International Gold Bullion Exchange, offered investors a solution for storage: The brothers would sell gold at a reduced price and store it in the company's vault. The investors, in fact, had to promise not to take delivery. That gave investors the opportunity to invest in gold but not be bothered with storage. The company's ads in major publications and on television and radio appealed to a lot of investors. In fact, the company sold about $125 million worth of gold.

Something about this arrangement didn't sound right to the authorities, however, and they began to look closely at the company. In their investigation, they decided to take a look at the gold the company had stored in its vault. When they went in, instead of finding $125 million worth of gold, they found five pieces of pinewood painted gold and a *Playboy* magazine. No real gold—no money. The company had only one real asset: its investor list. Scamsters from all over the country began trying to get the list of people who had invested with the International Gold Bullion Exchange in the hopes that they could scam the same people.

International Gold Bullion Exchange was running what's called a storage scam: An investor buys the commodity from the con artist, who supposedly takes possession of the goods and stores them. In reality, the con artist takes the investor's money but never purchases the commodity. This works well for the con artist because he gives the investor an official-looking piece of paper saying he has a certain amount of gold in storage, and the investor has no reason to call the con artist for months.

The only positive aspect to storage scams for the victims is that these types of scams are at least easy to understand. When it comes to other types of commodity investments, whether legitimate or fraudulent, the deals can become so complex and convoluted that even seasoned investors can become confused.

How Commodities Markets Work

The term *commodities* covers a wide range of products. There are agricultural products such as corn, coffee, and sugar. There are strategic metals such as gold, silver, and copper. There are energy commodities such as heating oil, gasoline, and natural gas. Even financial instruments such as treasury bills and bonds and stock indexes are considered commodities. The prices of these commodities can change rapidly due to weather conditions, economic conditions, and even political reasons, so these investments are highly volatile.

There are two ways you can invest in these commodities. First, commodities are traded as futures contracts—an agreement to buy or sell a certain amount of a commodity at a specific price at some date in the future—and you can buy and sell those contracts.

The second way is to buy and sell options on futures contracts. An option contract gives the investor the right, but not the obligation, to buy or sell a specified quantity of a commodity at a specific price within a specified period of time. The difference between these two forms of investment is obligation. Once you buy the futures contract, you are obligated. With an option, you don't have that obligation.

The purpose of the commodities market is to help the producers and users of these commodities to establish a market price. For instance, a farmer grows wheat and a baker uses flour made from the farmer's wheat. By setting a price for wheat several months into the future, the farmer can determine future income and the baker can plan for future expenses. Let's say the baker agrees to buy one thousand bushels of wheat at five dollars a bushel from the farmer on September 1. They enter into a contract, so regardless of what wheat is selling for in the open market on September 1, the baker will pay the farmer five dollars per bushel for one thousand bushels of wheat. If the market price on September 1 is higher than five dollars per bushel, the farmer loses because he could have sold his wheat on the open market for a higher price. If the market price is below five dollars per bushel on September 1, the baker loses because he could have purchased wheat in the open market at a lower price.

Producers and end users of commodities enter into futures contracts with the intent of taking delivery of the actual commodity. They use it as a form of insurance to control income and expenses. These buyers and sellers are called *hedgers*.

In fact, anyone can invest in these contracts because most futures contracts are traded on recognized exchanges, such as the Chicago Board of Trade, the New York Mercantile Exchange, and the Cotton Exchange. Therefore, other investors can trade these contracts purely as speculative investments without ever taking possession of the commodities behind the contracts. These people, who help to keep the market active, are called *speculators*.

Commodities can be highly risky because they're purchased on margin; the investor pays a minimal amount of money to control a much larger amount of the commodity. Therefore, small movements in price represent large changes in the value of the contract. With certain price fluctuations, investors can be called to add more money to their accounts. There are also various strategies that commodity traders employ that make investing in commodities even more complicated.

Enter the Con Artists

Con artists saw an opportunity in these markets and began running what are referred to as bucket shops. The con artists found potential victims through cold calling or by purchasing lead lists. When they got someone on the phone and convinced her to invest in commodities, the con artist would take the order, hang up, and throw the order in the garbage can, or bucket. In the meantime, the investor would send in her check to cover the purchase. The con artist would pocket the money and send back a phony statement. When the investor received the statement, she thought she was invested in the market.

The problem with bucket shops was that as soon as an investor called to liquidate her position and collect her money, she'd find there was no position and no money, and she'd call the authorities. The con artists would have to move and set up shop elsewhere to keep from being caught. Apparently they grew tired of running. Since then they have become more sophisticated. Instead of using lead lists and doing cold calling, they now advertise and run infomercials on television and radio. Some of their infomercials are even disguised as financial programs.

That's how a seventy-nine-year-old retired postal worker was taken in by a fraudulent investment company in December 1992. The man woke up in the middle of the night and couldn't sleep, so he turned on the radio to a Rochester, New York, radio station. He heard two men, who he thought were an independent financial adviser and a talk show host, discussing heating oil as an investment. The man subsequently called the 800 number provided and was told by the company representative that there were risks involved with the investment, but they were minimal. On December 28, 1992, the man sent in an account application and a check for ten thousand dollars to purchase options. One week later, the broker asked him to send another ten thousand dollars. He did. In August 1993, this retired postal worker closed his account and received a check for only $2,840—a loss of $17,160 in just eight months.

The National Futures Association (NFA) investigated, found the broker guilty of violations, and imposed sanctions that included a fine, a six-month suspension, activity restrictions for three years after the suspension, and a requirement to attend an ethics training course and sit for and pass the National Commodity Futures Examination.

When potential victims call the phone numbers broadcast in these types of commercials, they usually hear a sales pitch that totally distorts the truth about the investments the company is selling. The commodity markets are very fast to change course, are extremely speculative, and carry a lot of risk. Only sophisticated investors who are knowledgeable about the workings of these markets should invest in them. But these con artists don't talk about speculation and risk. Instead, they paint an exciting and rosy picture of almost certain huge returns and little risk.

Once they've convinced the investor that the commodity futures market is an easy way to make money, they open an account for the person, take orders for trades, and execute those trades. The trades they make are legal and legitimate, but the commission rates they charge are extremely high. That's how they make their money: extremely high rates of commission on lots of trades in lots of accounts. But to make sufficient amounts of money, they need to open a great number of accounts. Therefore, they have no regard as to the experience level, net worth, or other appropriate measures typically used in the industry to determine whether an investment is appropriate to the investor.

One broker convinced a widow with two sons to invest in oil and gas commodity futures and options, despite the fact that she told him she knew nothing about them. Another broker convinced a sixty-seven-year-old woman, who was provided her living expenses and a modest allowance by a religious organization, to invest in sugar options. The woman had no real income and a net worth equal to eighteen thousand dollars. And another pressured a man who said he had no experience in investing in stocks, mutual funds, or commodities into investing in sugar options. The broker said he preferred to work with first-time investors because he liked to train them.

Every one of these people was told that the commodity futures market was a great investment for them; in reality, it was probably the worst investment these people could have made. Convincing them to invest in commodities by using misleading sales solicitations and misleading advertisements and distorting the true risk level of the investment is illegal. But that doesn't stop the con artists. They're willing to tell any lie they can think of to make money. For the victims, however, it's hard to know if what they're being told is true. Not only does the story usually sound plausible, but the con artists harass their victims until they give in.

One couple was solicited by a company to invest in its Zero Basis Arbitrage Program. The couple told the salesperson they were not interested in commodities and had no money to invest. During the next several weeks, he called them numerous times. He told them that the program's risk level was very low—the next best thing to U.S. treasury bonds as a safe investment, he claimed. He explained that the only way they could lose money was in the event of a catastrophic event—say, such as the closing of Wall Street, World War III, or assassination of the president. He said there were no rational risks involved with the program. After weeks of these persistent calls, the couple agreed to open an account. During the first couple of weeks, they were told they were making money. After that, the losses came.

The information the broker gave these people as to the safety of this investment was completely false, because what they were investing in was more than risky—it was nonexistent. The company had no Zero Basis Arbitrage Program.

Protecting Yourself From Commodity Fraud

The commodity markets are highly sophisticated, extremely speculative, and highly dangerous and are best left to investors with experience.

In fact, legitimate marketers aren't even interested in dealing with retail customers who have only five thousand to ten thousand dollars to invest. Therefore, if someone talks to you about a futures investment of ten thousand dollars or less, be wary. The person may have someone else's interest in mind other than yours.

When an investor seeks to establish a futures trading account, the broker should ask questions as to the investor's income, net worth, and previous investment or futures trading experience. The broker should also supply the investor with written disclosure documents as to the risks involved with the investment and obtain written acknowledgment that the investor has received, read, and understands the information. Some brokers have been known to obtain all the required information from an investor, but then, through various means, convince the person to increase his or her income level on the application. Or the con artist will simply alter the information himself so the person appears to be a more appropriate investor than is really the case.

Investigating the Broker and the Firm

If you're considering doing business with someone offering commodity investments, check the person out. These products are traded on recognized exchanges, and the people and firms who sell them must be members of the NFA. The NFA, which was authorized by Congress and established on October 1, 1982, has the authority to enforce industry compliance and take disciplinary actions, such as fines and expulsion, against members when they violate the regulations.

Before investing, call the NFA at 1-800-621-3570 (within Illinois, call 1-800-572-9400) to find out if the person and firm are registered and legitimate. Or you can call the NFA's Disciplinary Information Access Line (DIAL) at 1-800-676-4NFA between 8:00 A.M. and 5:00 P.M. (central time). DIAL is a clearinghouse where investors can obtain disciplinary information about futures firms and salespeople. The information center receives more than 120,000 inquiries from member firms and the investing public each year, answering investors' questions and providing information as to disciplinary actions.

If the NFA reports that a company or salesperson has previous disciplinary actions, believe it. One woman called the NFA, just as she should have, after she was approached by a broker who wanted her to invest in sugar options. The NFA sent her a copy of a disciplinary complaint previously issued against the company. Instead of taking heed and walking away, she sent a copy of the complaint to the broker, who told her those types of complaints were very common in the investment field and that the complaint was no longer applicable because the company had corrected the errors. She believed him, invested, and lost most of her money.

There is one market in which you can't do much investigating before investing. That's the Foreign Exchange Market (Forex Market), which trades foreign currencies. For various reasons, no regulatory agency monitors this market, and because of this regulatory gap, it draws a lot of unsavory characters ready to sell any type of foreign currency contracts.

Their pitch is that foreign currencies, whether deutsche marks, Japanese yen, Swiss francs, or British pound sterling, are simple investments that can make you a great deal of money. When I requested material from one such company, I received a glossy, eighteen-page brochure complete with newspaper clippings from the *Wall Street Journal* that discussed what the Forex Market is, how it works, and the benefits of investing in foreign currency. A customer account agreement with envelope and prepaid Federal Express airbill were included so I could quickly and easily send them my deposit, which was required before I could enter into any transactions.

But I received no material about the company, its track record, or it principals and their backgrounds. When I called and asked for this information, I was told that it wasn't available. The company claimed that it couldn't give out track records because each investor's investment track record was different. According to the person I spoke to, no company ever publishes information about their principals. If I wanted to check the company out, however, I was told to call the Delaware Department of State, Division of Corporations. The person I spoke to even gave me the phone number. What he didn't say is that that organization is not a regulatory agency. All the Division of Corporations can confirm is whether the company is a Delaware corporation (and only for a ten-dollar fee). Being a Delaware corporation doesn't mean it's an honest company doing legitimate business.

I received three telephone calls from these people wanting me to invest. As soon as I told them I wouldn't invest until they supplied me with information about the company and its owners, I never heard from them again. When dealing with foreign currency investments, you're basically on your own, so be suspicious and make very careful and skeptical decisions.

"Well Known" Doesn't Mean "Honest"

But what if the principal of the company had been someone I had heard of before—maybe even someone well known? Would I have just assumed that everything was fine and made my investment? I hope not. The following story is sobering.

Russell Erxleben, who founded Austin Forex International in September 1997, was well known in sports circles; he was a three-time all-American kicker in the late 1970s for the Texas Longhorns football team at the University of Texas in Austin, Texas. (His record for the longest field goal in the school's history—sixty-seven yards—still stands.) He was a first-round draft pick of the New Orleans Saints in 1978 and played in the National Football League (NFL) for ten years.

Erxleben's Austin Forex International traded tens of millions of dollars of foreign currencies for investors until September 14, 1998, when the company abruptly closed its doors. According to a November 1, 1998, article in the *Austin American-Statesman*, state regulators claimed that Erxleben and Forex intentionally misled investors by not disclosing that the company was losing millions of dollars. The company was put in receivership while the state securities board, the FBI, and other regulatory agencies tried to sort out what had happened to investors' money. The article revealed that Erxleben had filed personal bankruptcy in 1991, had recently failed to pay federal taxes, was once indicted on felony bad-check charges, which were eventually dropped, and had been sued by the New Orleans Saints for a loan he didn't repay. The case is still under investigation, so no one knows if investors will get their money back. If investors had checked out Erxleben's background rather than being impressed by his past athletic feats, they might have saved themselves from going through the anxiety of this situation.

Erxleben isn't the only well-known person who has been accused of fraud. If you remember *The Mickey Mouse Club* television show, you probably remember Darlene, one of the original nine Mouseketeers. Darlene was found guilty of twelve counts of conspiracy, securities fraud, mail fraud, obstruction of justice, and perjury. On March 11, 1999, she was sentenced to 24 months' incarceration, 36 months' supervisory release, and a special assessment of $600. Don't let fame cloud your good judgment.

What to Do If You've Been Defrauded

If you find you've been defrauded in a commodity investment, report it to the NFA or your state securities agency. You can try reporting it to the broker's manager, but be careful. Remember the woman who called the NFA to find out about any disciplinary actions taken against a broker, then let the broker convince her that the actions reported didn't mean anything. At one point she became so frustrated with her losses that she demanded the broker adjust her account. He told her he had no authority to do so, but he would have someone who did have that authority call her. When the person called, he said he could not adjust her account, but he offered to switch her money from Eurodollars, where it was currently invested, to heating oil options, where he said she would get a better return. That transaction just generated more commissions for the broker. In total, the woman invested $9,400. During the time she invested with this company, she received one payment of $500. When she finally closed her account, she received $92.42—a loss of just over $8,800. Being one of the lucky victims, she eventually recovered her $8,800 in an arbitration hearing, but not without months of grief, worry, and frustration.

Almost two million futures contracts are traded on an average day. Just by the law of averages, it's inevitable that disagreements will arise between companies and their customers. If you find yourself in a dispute you can't resolve with the company you're working with, you can file a civil lawsuit, but there are easier and less expensive options. Call the NFA, ask for the compliance department, and report the problem. They'll offer you two options: mediation or arbitration.

As discussed in Chapter 18, during mediation a mediator assists the two parties by listening objectively to both sides and possibly suggesting ways of settling the dispute. Mediation sessions can be done over the telephone or in person, and the mediator may talk to the parties together or individually. In mediation, no one has to be proved wrong; the two parties must simply agree on a resolution. For claim amounts of less than $100,000, mediation is free, although there may be minimal expenses involved. Settlements are kept private and never disclosed to the public. You cannot, however, be forced to accept a settlement you don't agree to. Mediation is fairly quick and inexpensive.

If mediation doesn't work, arbitration is the next step. The arbitration process must be entered into before two years have passed since the disputed transaction occurred. There are certain fees charged to enter into arbitration, such as a filing fee, which is based on the dollar amount of the claim, a hearing fee, or a postponement fee. To enter into arbitration, you don't have to prove the company or salesperson broke any laws—only that they dealt with you unfairly. Decisions and awards determined through arbitration, however, are binding and cannot be appealed. The NFA has an average of 230 cases filed for arbitration each year, and almost 50 percent of NFA members and customers go through the process on their own without the help of an attorney. Since the NFA began offering the mediation process in 1991, there has been a dramatic increase in the number of arbitration cases settled prior to a hearing.

Ronald V. Hirst, Associate General Counsel and Enforcement Coordinator, National Futures Association, Chicago, Illinois

We worked on a case in which a woman with a net worth of only five thousand dollars heard a commodity investment ad on the radio. Instead of calling the number in the ad, she called a well-known old-line brokerage house. The broker told her that commodities were too risky for someone with her limited net worth and that she should put her money in the bank and not speculate in the commodity markets. He explained to her why these markets weren't right for her. That was exactly what he should have done. But she didn't listen. Instead, she got into a phone conversation with a broker at a less scrupulous firm who told her a lot of false and exaggerated information; she gave him her five thousand dollars, and it was gone. She never should have made the second call.

The point is that most commodity firms are legitimate and will be candid and forthright with people about the nature of the risks in commodity trading. But there are exceptions, and those people take a lot of money from people who can't afford to speculate in the commodity markets.

At NFA our goal is to protect the public from abusive sales and advertising practices. We've done a good job eradicating the more serious sales practice problems that were prevalent in the past, but con artists develop new ways of reaching people. For example, a few years ago, we hardly ever saw fraudulent television ads and infomercials touting commodities. Now they are a problem. We're currently developing new guidelines and rules that will reduce the problem ads.

The best way to avoid becoming a victim in a commodity scam is to be very wary of dealing with people over the phone and sending money to people you don't know. If someone calls you and wants you to invest in commodities but won't give you information about themselves or their companies, that's a red flag. Another red flag is if someone hypes dramatic profits and insists that you invest immediately. You have to be cautious and skeptical, and realize that if you don't have a good understanding of the inner workings of the commodity markets, which are extremely speculative, it's not an investment for you.

Checklist

Is the person:

- ❑ Encouraging you to purchase commodities and allow him to store them for you?

- ❑ Airing television or radio infomercials that appear to be financial programs?

- ❑ Painting a picture of certain success, huge returns, and little risk rather than addressing the true level of speculation and risk in commodity investments?

- ❑ Encouraging you to invest in the commodity markets despite your admission of having no experience?

- ❑ Offering you a commodity investment of ten thousand dollars or less?

- ❑ Encouraging you to invest in the commodity markets without discussing your income, net worth, or trading experience, or asking you to alter the information you supplied relative to your income level, net worth, or experience?

❑   Insisting you invest in foreign currencies but refusing to give you information about himself or his company?

If you answered yes to any of these questions, you're probably dealing with a con artist who specializes in commodity fraud.

PART FIVE

BUSINESS FRAUD

Sign Here and I'll Set You Up in Business: Franchise and Business Opportunity Fraud

The cynics are right nine times out of ten.

HENRY LOUIS MENCKEN, WRITER

Tired of taking orders from your boss? Tired of doing all the dirty work while your boss collects the big paycheck? You don't have to put up with any of that anymore. Now you can own your own day care center, be your own boss, and collect your own big paycheck.

Franchises

In 1995, some people accepted that opportunity from Tutor Time Child Care Systems, which was offering franchises for day care centers. Investors were told they could be their own boss by operating a day care center within eighteen months after paying their initial franchise fee. They could even get a day care center located in the geographic area of their choice. And the best part was that the promoter said most of the company's franchisees were earning a net income of at least $100,000 annually!

Unfortunately, some of those people were sorry they got

involved in this wonderful-sounding opportunity. In fact, they probably wished they were at their old jobs still taking orders from a boss. In 1996, the Federal Trade Commission (FTC) found the company was committing certain violations and imposed a civil penalty of $220,000 against the company. You see, there were a few problems.

The company did not tell potential franchisees that the individuals running the company had criminal backgrounds. They also failed to explain fully the terms and conditions of the financing arrangements, the length of time franchisees would have to wait between signing the franchise agreement and actually operating a franchise, and a few other details. Unfortunately for them, that's illegal under the FTC Franchise Rule.

According to Don DeBolt, president of the International Franchise Association, it's estimated that franchising will account for a trillion dollars in retail sales by the Year 2000. It's growing at a 10 to 12 percent pace per year as compared to gross domestic product growth of about 3 percent to 4 percent.

The popularity of franchising soared in the 1980s and 1990s for three reasons:

- *Awareness.* People have become more aware of the franchise option because franchise companies began advertising for potential franchisees on radio and television. There has also been an increase in the number of franchise trade expos and shows conducted across the country that potential investors can attend.

- *Downsizing.* In the past couple of decades, large numbers of employees have lost their jobs due to corporate downsizing. Many left their companies with severance pay packages, giving them available funds. For many, it was difficult to find comparable employment, so the answer was to become an entrepreneur and start a business of their own using their severance money. Franchising made that process easier.

- *Immigration.* Franchising used to be targeted at the average American, but the deluge of immigrants entering the country has become a new pool of potential franchisees. Often immigrants don't speak English well enough or understand the required legal procedures well enough to set up their own business. A franchise system gives them the assistance they need.

The classic franchise system is a company that for a fee offers individuals assistance in starting their own businesses. The franchisee has authority to use the company's trade name, which has value because it's recognizable. Franchisees are also given site location assistance, standard operating procedures, training, advertising, and a supplier of inventory. Because of all the assistance a good franchise system offers, buying in to one is a much easier way to go into business than trying to do all the legwork yourself. Moreover, franchises can be extremely profitable.

There's no standard method of franchising. Instead, it's based on a series of contractual obligations between the franchisee and the franchisor. The person who is buying (franchisee) is dependent on the representations and promises the seller (franchisor) offers. Therefore, the key for the con artist who is using the guise of franchising as a tool for running scams is to promise whatever is required to get investors to part with their money. If investors need training, that's what they're promised. If they're concerned about finding customers, the con artist promises to supply them.

The most common hook con artists use in franchise fraud is earnings misrepresentations. Buyers are told they'll earn a certain amount of money initially or within a certain time frame. Or they'll be told that current franchisees earn a certain average amount of money.

In the early 1990s, Tower Cleaning Systems, a commercial cleaning franchisor, promised potential franchisees that they could reasonably expect to achieve revenues as high as ten thousand dollars per month. The company, however, provided no earnings claims documentation to back up that statement and, in fact, did not even provide investors with the required disclosure document. The FTC filed a permanent injunction against it, and the company agreed to pay fifty thousand dollars in consumer redress.

The second most common hook is training claims. People who buy franchises often don't have the experience and expertise needed to start a business. Therefore, training is important to them.

For instance, how many of us would have the expertise needed to start a home-based travel agency? Probably not many. In

the early 1990s a franchise company told investors they could operate travel agencies in their own homes. The company promised
them access to and support from thousands of suppliers of travel
services, including airlines. Investors were also told they'd be
licensed or certified as travel agents pursuant to some "official
authority" and that they'd receive free computers and free or
deeply discounted travel opportunities. Investors were promised
$250,000 in annual sales and were told that previous investors had
a 100 percent success rate.

When these investors tried to start their travel agencies,
however, they got no assistance, no real certification, and no revenues in line with what was promised. Without training from the
company or support from airlines and other travel industry suppliers, how could these people possibly know where to begin?

When checking out a franchise offer, you may even be
given the names of current franchisees by the con artist so you can
interview them and ask about earnings claims, training, and other
promises. The FTC has seen innumerable cases where the references are people who may or may not have purchased a franchise,
but are paid shills who tell potential investors whatever the con
artist instructs.

When dealing with a bogus franchise operator, buyers may
find even after they've paid their money, besides receiving no assistance, training, or advertising, that competition is so strong that
there's no way they can ever earn back their investment, let alone
earn the kind of money the con artist promised.

Like other types of scams, the con artists follow the headlines. Whatever is hot in the marketplace is what the con artist is
selling. Con artists are currently pushing Internet franchises, such as
businesses that create Web pages, on-line malls, and other on-line
endeavors. People want to get in on the ground floor of a hot
industry, and the con artists take advantage of that.

Protecting Yourself From Franchise Scams

If you want to start your own business, a franchise is a great option
because it gives you the opportunity to be in business for yourself
but not by yourself. You do, however, have to take responsibility
for doing your homework and ensuring that you're investing with a

franchise system that is legitimate. There are several red flags you can look for that will pinpoint a scam:

- *Disclosure document.* All franchisors are required to supply potential franchisees with a disclosure document, called a Franchise Offering Circular, at least ten business days prior to the investor's signing a contract or paying any money. Although the FCC does not require this document to be filed with the commission, it does require franchisors to include information on twenty separate subjects—for example, identifying information about the franchisor, business experience of key personnel, description of the franchise, the cost to purchase a franchise, litigation history, and financial information about the franchisor. If the franchisor has not offered a disclosure document or isn't aware of the disclosure document requirement, there's a problem. Even if it isn't a fraudulent deal, the franchisor clearly doesn't know even the basics of franchising.
- *Business background.* Be sure the key executives have plenty of experience in franchising. If they're promising you the moon but have no experience, that's a red flag.
- *Litigation history.* Every company will have a lawsuit from time to time, but if being sued seems to be a regular practice, that signifies a problem. The FTC has seen disclosure documents that have eight to twelve single-spaced pages of descriptions of lawsuits the company is involved in, yet people invest nevertheless. This section of the disclosure document also includes information as to executives' past criminal activity, if applicable.
- *Turnover rate.* If a large percentage of franchisees have been in business for several years, that's a good sign. If instead franchisees come and go quickly, the franchisor isn't doing what it takes to make them happy and keep them in business. Get the names of some of the people who have left the system, call them, and find out why.
- *Earnings representations.* Although a franchisor isn't required to make earnings representations to potential buyers, many do. If they do, make sure those promises make sense and are substantiated. Is it just a number the salesperson threw out, or is it backed up with a valid basis and assumptions? Ask

what percentage of franchisees actually meet or exceed those earnings estimates. Get all earnings projections and other promises in writing.

• *High-pressure tactics.* The con artist will tell you the franchise offer is limited, or there is only one territory left, or this is a special one-time reduced franchise sales price. Don't be rushed. Take your time, read the disclosure document, and do your homework.

In addition to reading the disclosure document and having an adviser such as your accountant or attorney review the document, you should also visit the company's corporate headquarters. It's an investment in your future and certainly less costly than losing a complete franchise fee of thousands of dollars.

If you find yourself the victim of franchise fraud, ask the company to give your money back—although your chance of success is slim. Complain to the FTC. Although the FTC doesn't represent individuals and probably won't be able to get your money back, it can get injunctions that stop companies from their illegal conduct. Report problems also to the state regulatory officials and the state attorney general, or hire an attorney and file a lawsuit. The problem is that con artists don't usually hang around in one spot for very long. By the time you realize you've been duped, your money, and probably the con artist, will already be gone. Take time prior to investing to do the requisite research to ensure the franchise company you're doing business with is honest, trustworthy, and legitimate.

Business Opportunities

Want to get in on the ground floor of a really big discovery? In the early 1990s you could have had the opportunity to buy vending machines that dispensed the Alcohol Neutralizer, an herbal capsule that lowers blood alcohol levels by 50 percent in an hour. In fact, the company making this offer even said that the Harvard Medical School had run tests and found that the ingredients of the Neutralizer worked. Company representatives also said the capsule was perfectly safe because the federal Food and Drug Administration (FDA) had approved it. For forty-five hundred dollars, you could get five machines and install them in bars and restaurants where alcohol is served. Just think how much money you could make!

Small problem. The FDA had taken steps to stop the manufacture of the pill because an independent study conducted by an Indiana University scientist had found that the herbal ingredient in the pill could keep a person's blood alcohol level higher for a longer time than if the person had not taken the pill. Plus Harvard Medical School denied ever having done any research on this product.

This is what's known as a business opportunity scheme. There's a fine line of difference between a franchise and a business opportunity. Unlike a franchise, a business opportunity doesn't offer investors a trade name, operating manuals, or ongoing controls. Instead, the principals supply various types of machines plus the assistance of finding not only a location for those machines but also customers. Other business opportunity companies supply victims with software and customers for businesses operated out of the home. Business opportunity frauds fall into a few categories.

Vending Machines

> ### * * * EARN $5,000 A MONTH * * *
> Work part-time servicing a vending machine route
> Lucrative, High-Traffic Locations Available
> No selling/No experience necessary

The Claim
You buy the machines, and the company will place them in high-traffic, profitable locations. The most you have to do is clean and refill the machines, make sure they're in good repair, and collect money from the machines.

Reality
If the company actually installs the machines, chances are they'll be in remote locations where there are no customers. One such scam centers on ATMs. You buy the machine, and it is either leased back to you to generate rental income, or it's installed to generate

income from operations. Although the machines are actually sold, few leases are put in place, and the machines that are supposed to generate profit from operations are often placed in low-income-housing areas where most people don't even have ATM cards.

Rack Displays

WELL-KNOWN LICENSED PRODUCTS
Dealerships Now Available
$100,000 Annual Potential!!!
No experience necessary
Restock display racks at supermarkets, malls,
drugstores, and other retail outlets
Work part-time
Requires $14,000 to $46,000 investment

The Claim

All you have to do is restock display racks that retailers use to display products such as cosmetics, CDs, greeting cards, or other small items that you purchase from the promoter. The promoter will find locations for the racks, install them, keep them in good repair, and supply you with the merchandise to fill them. Your job is to keep them stocked.

Reality

You may end up with racks in an unprofitable area with the promoter supplying you with outdated merchandise that no one wants.

Medical Billing

MEDICAL BILLING BUSINESS
Work at home on your own computer
Earn $50,000 +/year!!!
No selling or experience required
We supply the doctors and dentists
Work full- or part-time

The Claim

You can do medical billing right in your own home. According to the promoter, doctors don't have time to handle their own billing, so the promoter will sell you the required software and supply you with doctors and dentists who want to outsource their billing.

Reality

The promoter doesn't supply you with any clients; you have to find your own. That's a difficult task because competition in medical billing is very strong and the industry is dominated by a few large, well-established companies.

Net-Based Businesses

* * * INTERNET OPPORTUNITIES * * *
Marketing Plans/Walk-Up Internet Access Machines/Seminars
Get in on the ground floor and
make money via the Internet
No computer experience necessary
Work at home!!!

The Claim

The company will sell you the opportunity to join its multilevel marketing plan so you can recruit people to sell devices that enable television access to the Internet. Or you can buy machines that give people in public places walk-up access to the Internet for a fee. Or you can pay thousands of dollars to take a seminar that teaches you how to make money on the Internet.

Reality
The multilevel marketing plan is an illegal pyramid scheme. The machines you buy are placed in low-traffic, unprofitable locations. The seminar is just a pitch for the company's Web site, which pushes other business opportunities.

Protecting Yourself From Franchise and Business Opportunity Scams

The North American Securities Administrators Association suggests the following ten tips to anyone who is considering investing in a franchise or a business opportunity:

1. If the franchisor doesn't give you a disclosure document, that's illegal. If he does, read it.
2. Have a trusted adviser, such as an attorney or accountant, review the deal before you sign documents or pay money. A list of consultants, including attorneys and accountants, and other helpful information can be found at the International Franchise Association's Web site at www.franchise.org.
3. Contact at least five people who have already invested and interview them about their experiences.
4. Consider that the references may be paid shills who will tell you what the promoter wants you to hear. Get the address of each franchisee's store or vending machine location, and check it out yourself. You should also visit the company's corporate head-quarters to be sure it exists.
5. Find out how many franchises were terminated in the past three years. If turnover is high, that's a sign of problems.
6. Make sure you understand the rules, such as what your daily business hours will be, how many employees you'll be required to hire, and other day-to-day details of operation.
7. Name recognition is a big part of joining a franchise system. If you've never heard of this company, it may not be worth pur-chasing.

8. Determine how the site selection process works. A poorly selected site will probably mean failure.
9. Be sure you understand the level of training you'll receive. If you don't know how to operate the business and the franchisor doesn't provide the training you need, you'll have a problem.
10. Check out the company and its executives with the Better Business Bureau, consumer protection agency, state securities agency, or state attorney general. They can tell you about any past disciplinary actions.

When dealing with someone who wants to help set you up in your own business, don't fall prey to high-pressure sales tactics, the promises of exorbitant profits, claims of no risk, or unjustified start-up fees. Be sure your questions are answered clearly and fully, and to your satisfaction.

For helpful information on judging a franchise, visit the FTC's Web site at www.ftc.gov for news releases, business guidance, and consumer protection information. You can also call the FTC at 1-202-326-2222, or write to it at Public Reference, Federal Trade Commission, Washington, D.C. 20580 to order "Best Sellers," a complete list of the FTC's consumer publications. The more information you have and the better you understand franchising and business opportunities, the more likely you'll succeed in finding one that's right for you.

The whole point of going into business for yourself is to make money. Take time and care to be sure the one making money is you, and not a con artist.

Don DeBolt, President, International Franchise Association, Washington, D.C.

If someone is interested in becoming involved in a franchise but isn't certain which franchise fits his needs, he may want to attend a franchise show. An expo is an opportunity for prospective franchisees to experience one-stop shopping to review the various franchise concepts that are available. There are probably a couple of dozen expos across the country annually, most ranging in size from thirty to forty exhibitors.

Every spring in Washington, D.C., IFA sponsors the International Franchise Expo, the largest in the country with approximately 350 exhibitors. Before a franchisor can exhibit at our expo, we prescreen them to ensure they're complying with federal and state disclosure requirements. We draw almost twenty thousand potential franchisees and get thirty or forty overseas delegations attending.

With 350 exhibitors to choose from, attendees need to have a sense of the type of franchise they're interested in and narrow their scope to a few before they come to the expo. For example, if they are interested in a restaurant franchise, do they want a full-service restaurant or fast food? If they want fast food, would they prefer to sell Mexican food, hamburgers, or chicken?

We encourage people to request a list of exhibitors beforehand so they can study it and have an idea of which franchises to focus on. They should also have a basic list of questions to ask each franchisor. If they need assistance in compiling appropriate questions, they can order our *Franchise Opportunities Guide* for $21 including shipping by calling us at 1-800-543-1038.

When attendees get to the expo, I recommend they rapidly walk the show first to get a sense of the layout. They then need to talk to the exhibitors whose franchises they're interested in. Many exhibitors have one or two of their franchisees on hand whom attendees can talk to. Gather as much information as you can; then go home and study it, talk to your family, call current and former franchisees, obtain and review the disclosure documents, contact your attorney and business adviser or accountant, and visit the franchisor's headquarters and training facilities to get a sense of the company and its culture and how you might fit in.

A franchise expo is a great opportunity to make initial contacts and start the process of finding an appropriate franchise. Keep in mind, however, that an expo is a sales environment. Don't get caught up in the hoopla and make a snap decision. Buying into a franchise requires a large investment and always involves risk. Be certain a franchise is right for you before you commit. I can't repeat it often enough: Investigate before you invest.

Checklist

Is the salesperson:

❑ Claiming you can make huge profits owning a specific franchise but can't substantiate that claim with a valid basis and assumptions?

❑ Encouraging you to invest in a franchise, but not supplying you with the required Franchise Offering Circular?

❑ Charging extremely high start-up fees to open a franchise?

❑ Being sued by a large number of previous franchisees?

❑ Showing huge turnover in his franchisee base?

❑ Pressuring you into making a quick decision?

❑ Claiming you can make a huge salary by working part-time in a vending machine, rack display, medical billing, or other business?

If you answered yes to any of these questions, this franchise or business opportunity offer may be fraudulent.

CHAPTER 11

When Employees Take Home More Than Their Paychecks

I'm living so far beyond my income that we may almost be said to be living apart.

E. E. CUMMINGS, POET, WRITER, AND PAINTER

Steve was nineteen years old when he began working as a shipping clerk at a computer microprocessor chip manufacturing plant. Every day he handled thousands of chips and often wondered how much each one was worth. He decided to find out. While at work one day, he slipped one of the chips from a barrel and stuffed it in his pocket. When he showed the chip to Ron, his girlfriend's father, who operated a computer salvage business, he told him the chip had been discarded as scrap. Ron estimated the chip to be worth about forty dollars.

Steve asked Ron if he knew anyone who might be interested in buying scrap chips. He said he did. Shortly after, Steve stole three boxes of chips from his employer by loading them on a cart and piling empty boxes on top and passing the security guards under the guise of taking empty boxes to the trash outside. Once in the parking lot, he put the three full boxes in his trunk. He sold them for five thousand dollars.

Two weeks later, Steve stole four more boxes of chips and received ten thousand dollars for them. Excited about the easy money, he told a co-worker about his thefts and offered to split the profits with him if he would help remove the boxes of chips from the plant. The co-worker agreed to help steal six more boxes in order to split the fifty thousand dollars Steve had been promised by his purchaser. Steve took the six boxes home, removed the company labels from the boxes, and delivered them to his purchaser, who promised to pay him the fifty thousand dollars within a few days.

What Steve and his coworker didn't know was that management was aware that boxes of chips had been stolen, but they didn't know who the thief was. Without telling employees, the company improved its inventory control procedures and installed additional surveillance cameras around the factory.

When Steve and his co-worker came to work the day after stealing the six boxes of chips, they were confronted with the evidence of the theft, and the pair confessed. They gave police the name of their purchaser, but when police arrested him, he had already sold the chips for a whopping $697,000.

Steve served over a year in the state penitentiary for grand theft and embezzlement, and his co-worker got nine months in a work furlough program. The company wasn't able to recover its inventory, but management did learn an expensive lesson. The plant now has tighter controls and physical security, and it conducts more frequent inventory audits.

When you own your own business, you can expect to lose a few dollars to employee abuse. Employees may take a pen or a box of paper clips home. They may come to work late, leave early, or stretch out a lunch hour. Employees may call in sick when they're perfectly healthy, or squeeze a few extra dollars out of their expense account reimbursements. These abuses can become fairly expensive. But petty theft isn't the type of abuses that employers fear most.

In a two-and-a-half-year study, the Association of Certified Fraud Examiners in Austin, Texas, learned much about the dynamics of occupational fraud and abuse. According to Joseph T. Wells, the association's chairman and founder, there are three primary types of frauds that employees perpetrate against their employers:

asset misappropriations, bribery and corruption, and fraudulent statements.

Asset Misappropriations

This type of employee fraud, which represents just over 80 percent of frauds committed against employers, involves an employee's stealing or misusing the company's assets for his own benefit. Approximately 90 percent of the time, these misappropriations involve stealing cash; the other 10 percent involves the misappropriation of inventory or other assets, such as supplies, equipment, or information. Although the misappropriation of assets other than cash represents a minimal number of crimes committed, the loss associated with each of those crimes is twice as much as the loss involved in the average cash misappropriation crime. Three types of crimes fall under asset misappropriation.

Skimming

The crime of skimming involves an employee's making a sale and converting the money to his own use before the sale gets recorded in the books. For example, someone who works in a fast-food restaurant may sell $10.85 worth of food, collect the money, hit the No Sale button on the cash register, and pocket the money. The manager never knows the sale took place because the $10.85 sale was never recorded.

Another way some bold employees skim money is by operating their employer's business during nonbusiness hours. One manager of a retail facility would open the store he managed at 8:00 A.M. instead of 10:00 A.M. as he was supposed to, and would pocket all the money he made during those two extra hours of business. His employer didn't know the employee was stealing from him because he didn't even know his store was open during those hours.

Larceny

Larceny involves stealing money with no real attempt to cover up the crime. In committing larceny, the employee who stole $10.85 from the fast food restaurant would make the sale, collect the money, ring it up on the cash register, then pocket the money. Or maybe he rings up sales all day long and then at the end of the day reaches in the register and steals one hundred dollars. Because cash larceny crimes are fairly easy for management to detect, some employees devise ways to cover up the crime. For instance, in some retail organizations, employees are assigned to specific cash registers. The thief may steal money from another employee's cash register to cover up his tracks and implicate the other employee. Employees may also use reversing transactions by processing false voids or refunds so the cash register tape reconciles to the amount of cash on hand after the theft.

Fraudulent Disbursements

These types of crimes involve a little more work on the part of the criminal. In a fraudulent disbursement crime, the employee may create fraudulent expense accounts that are paid directly to him. Or he may create a dummy company that he controls. He then writes corporate checks to that company.

Corruption

This category, which represents 10 percent of employee crime, requires the assistance of an accomplice who works outside the company. There are four types of corruption that employees perpetrate against employers: bribery, conflict-of-interest schemes, economic extortion schemes, and illegal gratuities schemes. The study by the Association of Certified Fraud Examiners found that bribery represented 89 percent of corruption crimes, and conflict-of-interest schemes represented 9 percent.

Bribery

In perpetrating bribery, an employee may make a deal with a supplier to inflate invoices by 10 percent. They then split the extra profit. Or an employee may agree to give all the company's business to one supplier who agrees to give him a 10 percent kickback for his consideration. Typically bribery consists of kickbacks and bid-rigging schemes. For example, a purchasing agent at one retail company agreed to book all corporate travel through one specific travel agent. In return, the travel agent provided him with free travel and entertainment. The victimized company calculated that it paid ten thousand dollars more in travel expenses in a two-year period than it should have due to the employee's bribery scheme.

Conflict-of-Interest Schemes

Fairly high level executives are typically the perpetrators of conflict-of-interest schemes. The way it works is that an executive may own a company or have an interest in a company that produces a product that his employer uses. For instance, a person may work at a company that manufactures clocks and be part owner of a company that manufactures the hands used on clocks. When selling those hands to his employer, he may inflate the price substantially.

Economic Extortion Schemes

In economic extortion, the opposite of bribery, someone requires a bribe from you as a condition of doing business. For instance, as a business owner, you may approach a bank about a loan to fund an upcoming expense or an expansion. When you apply to borrow the money, the loan officer tells you that in order for him to approve the loan, he expects you to pay him a kickback.

In one case, a manager for a utility company started his own business on the side. He then forced vendors to divert some of their business to his company if they wanted him to award them work with the utility company.

Illegal Gratuity Schemes

Illegal gratuities involve an employee's accepting a reward for giving a certain vendor a specific part of the company's business. It's similar to bribery except that something of value is given to an employee to reward a decision rather than to influence it. For example, an employee who's in charge of finding a paper supplier may give one company all the business. At the end of the year, in gratitude, that vendor may give the employee a free vacation or other expensive gifts.

Fraudulent Statements

This category, which represents less than 10 percent of employee crime, is typically carried out by a high-level executive or even the owner of the company. In order to obtain funding, sell stock, or receive other assistance, the executive or owner may tamper with the corporate books to make it appear that the company's performance is better than it really is. Through various means, he'll increase the amount of assets or income on the books or reduce the amount of money the company owes to show a favorable financial position.

One of the more flamboyant of these fraudulent statements types of fraud was ZZZZ Best carpet cleaning service founded by Californian Barry Minkow, who started the business in his parents' garage when he was a high school junior in the mid-1980s. Minkow inflated numbers in the corporate books and created bogus accounts to impress clients and potential investors. Based on those falsified books, the company went public on the New York Stock Exchange in 1986, raising twelve million dollars. Minkow used some of the money to pay off early investors and some lenders, but most of the money disappeared. Everything fell apart when the *Los Angeles Times* published an article stating that Minkow was a credit card scam artist. Securities investigators began to look into the company, and it quickly fell apart. Minkow was sentenced to twenty-five years in a federal prison in Colorado. He was released in 1996 after serving eighty-seven months. These types of employee crimes cross over to become micro-cap stock frauds in which unsuspecting investors buy stock in a bogus company. The investing public bears the brunt of this crime.

Another type of fraudulent statements crime involves professionals who misstate their credentials to their employers. For example, we've all heard the story about the surgeon who has been performing surgeries for a hospital, but never went to medical school or college, and never even finished high school.

Protecting Yourself From Occupational Fraud

According to the Association of Certified Fraud Examiners, small companies—those with one hundred or fewer employees—are one hundred times more likely than larger companies to experience fraud from within. That fraud is almost always a situation of misplaced trust in the people who handle the company's money. That's because small companies often have one-person accounting departments, leaving that person free to do as he or she pleases, with no checks and balances. Having the same person keep the books and write the checks is giving that person an invitation to steal money.

The Association of Certified Fraud Examiners estimates that the annual cost to U.S. organizations from occupational fraud and abuse totals more than $400 billion—six times the cost of operating the U.S. criminal justice system. Typically the perpetrators of these crimes are college-educated white males. In fact, they found that women committed only one-quarter of all crimes. Most people who steal from their employers start out filching small amounts. Because it's so difficult to detect those types of thefts, the person can steal small sums of money over long periods of time. But when those thefts go undetected, the person tends to steal more and more. As the size of the thefts increases, the signs become more obvious. One prevalent sign is the flaunting of money, such as the bank teller who began taking her fellow employees to lunch in a limousine. Most people who steal from their employees say that once they start, they can't stop. They also typically believe they are morally justified in stealing—the company owes them for some wrong, or they tell themselves they'll someday pay it back.

It's extremely difficult for management, or even the company's auditors, to detect employee fraud because it's so subtle. Therefore, the best option is to stop fraud before it starts. The Association of Certified Fraud Examiners suggests the following guidelines:

- Set an example. Employees who view their employers as being honest will emulate that behavior and vice versa.
- Implement a written code of ethics that states what the company expects from its employees. If you don't have anyone internally who can perform this function, there are consultants who offer this service. Check with your accounting or law firm for suggestions.
- Prescreen applicants by checking references and performing background checks. A legal office hired a bookkeeper who wrote twenty-two checks totaling $186,000 to herself and forged the law partner's signature. The fraud was discovered after she resigned. The law partner then learned the woman had two prior embezzlement convictions and had served four

years in prison. She went on to steal from two more employers. Any one of those employers could have eliminated the problem by making a background check.

- Don't have one person keep the books and write the checks. Separate those duties.

- Know who your suppliers are. If your purchasing person shows favoritism to one supplier or buys all your products from a single source, ask why.

- Insist that monthly bank statements be delivered unopened to a high-level executive who is unconnected to bank reconciliations to deter skimming cash and making false disbursements. Look for names you don't recognize, unusual patterns, dual endorsements, and unfamiliar financial trends.

- Create a positive workplace so that employees don't have any motivation for revenge.

- Pay attention to customers who complain about being dunned for invoices they've already paid.

- Ensure that your computer system is set up so that only the people who require access to various areas have that access. Companies have experienced employees illegally using company computer systems to steal telephone credit card numbers, get access to bank account numbers, and manipulate billings.

- Hire the right people, treat them well, and don't subject them to temptation. If you hire the right person and put him in the wrong circumstances where your primary control is blind trust, even a good person may not be able to overcome that temptation.

- Don't think that because someone earns a good salary, that person won't steal from you. And if he does, and is prosecuted, the problem may not end there. The president of United Way of America was earning more than $463,000 a year in salary and benefits when he was caught stealing $1.2 million from the charity's till. He was sentenced to seven years in prison. Three years after sentencing, a federal judge ruled that despite his conviction and prison sentence, the charity must pay him $2 million in retirement benefits due him!

- If a disgruntled employee leaves or is fired, change computer passwords, and be sure you have a good computer security system in place. Always back up computer files, keep backup copies off-site, and be sure you have an effective anti-virus computer program.

- Be sure your employees know whom they should contact if they uncover a problem or suspect a co-worker of fraud. Many frauds are caught due to tips from other employees or even complaints from vendors.

- Check addresses of vendors against addresses of employees. If you uncover matching addresses, you've probably found a phony vendor.

- Have adequate amounts of bonding against employee dis-honesty. In most cases, insurance is affordable and will keep you from having a catastrophic loss.

- Pay attention to employees who come to work early, stay late, and never take a vacation. Perpetrators know that frauds are most often uncovered when the person is away.

If you believe you've become the victim of employee fraud, be very careful in how you handle your suspicions. Wrongfully accusing an employee of theft can open you up to major liability. If you can release an employee for other legitimate reasons, such as poor performance, that's your best bet. If you do accuse an employee of theft, you had better have those accusations docu-mented completely. Never accuse someone based on your suspi-cions.

Even if you do catch a thief, the truth is that most people who steal from their employers are never prosecuted. The police are reluctant to follow up on occupational fraud cases. They're too busy chasing robbers and drug dealers and often believe that if the company had its house in order, the theft never would have hap-pened. The disinterest of the authorities is equally balanced, how-ever, by employers' reluctance to prosecute. They don't want to admit they have thieves working for them, and once they turn the case over to police, the story will appear in the newspapers and maybe even on the local television or radio news. Chances are great that any money the employee has stolen has already been spent, so it's nearly impossible to recover any losses anyway. Most employers just get rid of the problem and write off the losses. That creates another problem.

Because of the fear of litigation, employers aren't willing to disclose that they fired someone because that person was stealing from the company. Therefore, those employees are turned back into the workplace to steal from their next employer.

Employee fraud will never be eliminated; the controls and monitoring it would take would be cost prohibitive. But it can be reduced if employers and business owners take the time to check the references of potential employees thoroughly, establish controls that work, use physical security to the extent needed, and pay attention to what's happening throughout the company. The time spent could avert a devastating loss: the potential loss of the whole company, and, therefore, every employee's livelihood and every shareholder's investment.

Barry Minkow, Senior Pastor, Community Bible Church, San Diego, California

Sentenced to twenty-five years for securities fraud, mail fraud, bank fraud, and tax evasion.

Served eighty-seven months in prison.

At the high school I went to, if you weren't the star football player, didn't have good looks, or didn't have a lot of money, you didn't have a date. The first two didn't work out for me, which left money. I was driving a 1972 Buick and knew I needed to get money to buy a new car so I could have a social life.

When I was sixteen years old, I was cleaning carpets and doing a good job, so I decided to start a carpet cleaning business. I called it ZZZZ Best. I operated the company for five years and ultimately had twenty-three offices with fourteen hundred employees. The company never made any money and eventually was in dire circumstances. But I couldn't go to my employees and tell them I couldn't make payroll and admit I was a failure as a leader. For me, to admit failing was more difficult than to commit a crime. So I kited checks, stole money orders, inflated insurance claims, and borrowed money under false pretenses. I even raised twelve million dollars through an initial public offering by lying about having customer contracts and a certain level of revenues. I convinced myself that lying to get money was all right because I was eventually going to pay it all back anyway. I never intended to defraud anyone.

By December 1986 I had raised about thirty million dollars in cash. If my motive had been to take the money and run, I would have done it then. But I didn't. I used the money to operate the company, make television commercials, and open new offices. I don't know why I didn't understand that if we weren't profitable with fifteen offices, we'd never be profitable with twenty-three offices. The end came when the auditors insisted on physically seeing restoration jobs I'd told them we were working on but didn't really exist.

I never planned at age sixteen to defraud Wall Street by the time I was twenty. But by making bad choices, that's what happened. When I realized I was a crook, that I wouldn't be able to pull it off any longer, and that people would be financially harmed, it had a devastating affect on my life. That guilt led me to Christ and the Christian faith.

Everyone says about prisoners, "You're born again until you're out again." But I've proved over time that's not true. The prison guidelines say that for my crime, I should have spent forty to fifty-two months in prison. I spent eighty-seven months in prison. I've since acquired a master of arts in religion and a master of divinity degree. I'm a pastor of Community Bible Church in San Diego, I give speeches on fraud prevention, and I have a radio show called *Consumer Hotline*, which focuses on fraud. I've lived an honest life since my release and plan to continue to do so. My skeptics have even come to admit that I'm on the right path because authenticity is verified by consistency.

The victims of my crime have received about 95 percent of their money back, primarily from a shareholder lawsuit filed against the lawyers and accountants for negligence. One bank is still out about seven million dollars. Every time I get paid for a speaking engagement, I split the money with the bank. It's modest, but to them it's ownership of responsibility twelve years after the fact.

When people say, "Once a con man, always a con man," they are just out of touch. I'm convinced that Christ can change lives. I've seen it in myself and others. People can change because Christ transforms them from the inside out so that they're not victims of their genes or their past. We have the ability as Christians to be victorious over a propensity to deceive.

Checklist

Does your company:

- ❏ Have one person keep the books and write the checks?
- ❏ Have employees who flaunt wealth beyond their means?
- ❏ Have employees who come to work early, stay late, and never take vacations?
- ❏ Receive complaints from customers about being dunned for bills that they've already paid?
- ❏ Allow computer access to employees who really don't need that access?
- ❏ Leave computer passwords intact after a disgruntled employee has been fired?
- ❏ Have no procedures for conducting background checks on new employees?
- ❏ Show favoritism to one supplier?

If you answered yes to any of these questions, you may be the victim of employee fraud.

PART SIX

OTHER TYPES OF FRAUD

CHAPTER 12

There Are Two of You Now: Identity Theft

We have no right to ask, when sorrow comes, Why did this happen to me? unless we ask the same question for every joy that comes our way.

PHILIP S. BERNSTEIN

When Helen had her wallet stolen, she knew it would be a hassle to replace her driver's license, credit cards, and other personal items, but she didn't view it as a major problem. That was before she was arrested. The woman who stole her wallet went to Nevada, had an identification made with Helen's personal information but her own photo, and then committed a crime. The police ended up with Helen's name as the perpetrator of the crime, and she was arrested. She managed to straighten out the mix-up and get released from jail, but now she's having difficulty renting an apartment because every time a potential landlord submits her Social Security number for a credit check, two names come up.

Paulette, a young mother of a twenty-month-old child, found that an imposter obtained her Social Security number, date of birth, and mother's maiden name. With that information, the woman got credit in Paulette's name and purchased a $40,000 motor home and ran up other bills totaling more than $100,000.

While going through the security check at the airport, Gina's wallet was stolen. In just four hours, $10,000 had been charged to her credit card. Gina cancelled her credit cards, but because of the black mark the incident made against her credit report, she now can't get a loan to buy a house. Even worse, after the thief stole the wallet, she went to another state and gave birth to a child using Gina's name and identification. Gina is now listed on the birth certificate as being the mother of that child.

These three people are victims of identity theft: stealing someone's personal information such as a Social Security number, date of birth, bank account numbers, or mother's maiden name. With that information, the thief can create havoc with the victim's credit rating, reputation, and life.

Victims of identity fraud can face years of trying to clear their creditworthiness. In the meantime, they may not be able to find a job, rent an apartment, buy a house or car, or obtain other types of loans such as tuition loans to send their children to college. The victim whose identity is stolen isn't the only victim. The companies that grant credit, such as banks, credit card companies, and retailers, are also victims because they extend credit that is never paid. According to a Government Accounting Office (GAO) report, *Identity Fraud: Information on Prevalence, Cost, and Internet Impact Is Limited*, the dollar losses related to identity fraud reported by MasterCard and Visa alone in 1997 were $407 million and $490 million, respectively.

Identity theft can be one of the most devastating types of fraud perpetrated. Not only may victims not even know they're victims until tremendous damage has been done, but chances are good that they'll never find out who the perpetrator was. One woman who had her identity stolen and fought it for ten years had the opportunity to see a picture of her imposter. The imposter was over fifty years old, weighed more than two hundred pounds, and sported tattoos. The victim was considerably younger, weighed much less, and had no tattoos. Despite the physical differences, when the con artist was jailed twice for convictions for driving under the influence, the victim had to go to court and be fingerprinted to prove she was not the person who was driving under the influence.

The Identity Thief's Modus Operandi

Thieves obtain the information they need by finding it in computerized databases; looking through dumpsters for bank deposit slips, preapproved credit card offers, or other discarded documents; stealing your wallet; stealing your mail right out of your mailbox; or even bribing employees of companies who have access to customer or personnel records. They can obtain your credit report directly from a credit bureau by posing as an employer, loan officer, or landlord. Information found on your credit report includes your Social Security number and a list of your credit cards and their numbers.

With this information, they can rent an apartment in your name, establish services with utility companies, change your address with your credit card companies, establish credit, create debt, take over your existing financial accounts, apply for governmental benefits, and assume your complete identity, even putting you in jeopardy relative to any illegal acts the person may commit.

Chuck Whitlock, an investigative reporter, wanted to find out how difficult it would be to steal someone's identity and how much damage could be done. His friend Brent Collier, chief of police in Milwaukie, Oregon, agreed to help by allowing Chuck to go through his garbage. In the garbage, Chuck found a bank deposit slip, a utility bill, and a receipt for payment on an insurance policy.

With those three pieces of identification, he went to the Department of Motor Vehicles, posed as Brent, and said he lost his driver's license. He was issued a new license with his picture and Brent's name. He then went to a check-printing company and used the bank deposit slip to have two hundred blank checks printed with Brent's name and account number on them. With the driver's license and checks, he rented a penthouse suite in an apartment complex under Brent's name. When the landlord said she'd have to run a credit check on him, he asked if he could get a copy of the credit report if he paid the fee. That credit report supplied him with a list of Brent's credit cards and their numbers.

Chuck called the credit card companies and asked them to reissue the credit cards to his new address. With the credit cards reflecting the new address, he had the ability to purchase merchandise over the phone and have it sent directly to him. He also purchased jewelry in a store and paid for it with the checks he had printed. In the end, he made twenty-four thousand dollars' worth of purchases in Brent's name. If he had been an actual con artist, he could have continued the identity fraud and created even more problems for his victim.

The Con Man's Newest Scam

Although the amount of identity fraud committed is increasing, most of the perpetrators go unpunished. According to the GAO report, Trans Union Corporation, one of the national credit bureaus, received 522,922 inquiries regarding identity theft in 1997. That was up from 35,235 just five years earlier. But the Secret Service reports that there were only 9,455 arrests for these types of crimes under its jurisdiction in 1997. Many retailers write off fraud rather than pursue the criminals because the legal fees would be more than the value of the lost merchandise. And the people whose identities have been stolen can't press charges in many states because *they* are not considered the victims; the banks or stores that lose money are considered the victims and are the only ones who can press charges. If their loss isn't substantial, chances are, they'll write it off rather than spend money to prosecute, and the con artist goes free.

When identity theft con artists are caught, the consequences are usually fairly minor. It's not a violent crime, and prison space is limited, so they end up with a sentence of parole or community service. For those who do get jail time, it's usually just six months or a couple of years, but they get released in half the time and start working their con again. Most identity theft criminals, however, are never caught and prosecuted because these crimes are infrequently even investigated.

According to Beth Givens, director of the Privacy Rights Clearinghouse, a consumer information and advocacy program in California, the lack of consequences that identity thieves face has caught the eye of plenty of criminals who look for easy ways to make money. Banks have become fairly effective at thwarting armed robbers, and the penalties for robbing at gunpoint are stiff, so criminals who used to rob banks have turned to identity theft because it's easier, there's less chance of being caught, and if they are caught, the consequences are minor. Organized crime rings, and even the Russian Mafia, raise money for their criminal activities by committing identity theft.

The Consequences for the Victim

Victims of identity theft may not even know they are a victim. It can take months before they realize they have a problem. Most victims discover the theft in one of three ways:

- *Refusal for credit.* The victim applies for credit to buy a house or a car or to refinance a mortgage and finds he has bad credit because the con artist ran up debts under his name.
- *Collection agency calls.* Credit grantors, such as department stores, turn over their late accounts receivable to collection agencies that seek out the debtors. While the con artist is making the charges, the collection agency finds the real person and harasses her to pay the bill. The victim may not even have a credit card with the company in question.
- *Credit card company calls.* Most large credit card companies have developed sophisticated computer profiling systems that can detect out-of-character charges. When that happens, the victim receives a call from someone at the credit card company, who informs the victim that there is a pattern of activity on her credit card that is inconsistent with past purchases.

Fortunately, the victim is not liable for paying the bills an identity theft creates. The law says the victims of credit card fraud are liable for only fifty dollars, but most credit card companies even waive that liability. Most other types of credit grantors also waive liability as soon as they verify that a victim is innocent. Debit card issuers, while not bound by the fifty dollars liability rule, have voluntarily agreed to honor the law that relates to credit cards.

Of course, there are monetary consequences tied to the victim's inability to rent an apartment, obtain credit, or find employment. Once the victim's identity has been stolen and the damage done, it can take years to resolve the problem. In 1993, someone in California collected eleven thousand dollars in unemployment benefits under Raul's Social Security number. Raul, who lived in the Midwest, learned of the problem in 1996 when he was laid off, tried to collect benefits, and was denied. When Raul found employment again, the California Employment Development Department threatened to garnish his wages, accusing him of collecting unemployment benefits in California in 1993 when at the same time he was employed in the Midwest. Trying to prove innocence can be frustrating. In Raul's case, for him to have committed the crime he was accused of, he would have to have been in two places at the same time. It should have been simple to resolve, but it wasn't.

Some identity thefts continue to such extreme ends that the thief has thirty or forty credit cards in the victim's name and has bought a house in his name, and the victim is constantly harassed by collection agencies. Some victims reach the point of such sheer frustration and inability to deal with the problem that they file for bankruptcy to relieve themselves of the burden. The Privacy Rights Clearinghouse, however, recommends that victims never file bankruptcy as a result of identity theft. In fact, even bankruptcy may not get rid of the con artist. Not all credit grantors do a good job of checking credit reports for bankruptcy filings. Therefore, the imposter may still be able to obtain credit in the victim's name. Also, a bankruptcy remains on the victim's credit report for years. Just ask Bernard. Someone filed bankruptcy in his name; now Bernard can't buy a house because the bankruptcy filing keeps showing up on his credit report.

On October 30, 1998, President Clinton signed into law the Identity Theft and Assumption Deterrence Act of 1998, which makes it a federal crime to illegally obtain or use another individual's means of identification. The law sets criminal penalties and provides for mandatory restitution for identity fraud victims.

The Department of Justice is charged with enforcement of the law, but its resources are stretched to the limit, forcing it to prioritize which types of crimes it investigates and prosecutes. Time will tell if identity crimes will take high enough priority to make a difference, despite new legislation.

Protecting Yourself From Identity Theft

The best strategy is to take steps that can help protect you from identity theft. The first step is to find out if you've already become a victim by ordering copies of your credit report from the three credit reporting agencies twice a year:

Equifax
P.O. Box 105873
Atlanta, Georgia 30348
1-800-685-1111

The letter requesting your report from Equifax should include your full name, current address and former address if you haven't been at your current address for two full years, Social Security number, date of birth, and day and evening phone numbers. You must also include a copy of your driver's license or a utility bill and an eight-dollar check in most states. Or you can order the report directly over the phone and charge it to your credit card.

Trans Union Corp.
Merchants Association Credit Bureau
P.O. Box 3307
Tampa, Florida 33601
1-813-273-7700

The letter requesting your report from Trans Union should include your name, current address and former address if you haven't been at your current address for two full years, Social Security number, date of birth, day and evening phone numbers, and name of your employer. You must also include an eight-dollar check in most states. You cannot get this report over the phone using a credit card.

Experian
P.O. Box 2104
Allen, Texas 75013-2104
1-800-682-7654

The letter requesting your report from Experian should include your full name, current address and former addresses if you haven't been at your current address for five full years, Social Security number, and date of birth. You must also include a copy of your driver's license or a utility bill and an eight-dollar check in most states. Or you can order the report directly over the phone and charge it to your credit card.

You can obtain all three reports free of charge if you meet certain conditions. Call the toll-free numbers listed prior to sending your letters and listen to the recording to determine if you qualify to receive the report free of charge. You should order these reports at least twice a year to ensure no fraud has occurred.

The next call you should make is to the Opt Out Request Line, at 1-888-567-8688. Over the phone, you can supply your full name, address, Social Security number, and phone number. It will then remove your name from lists of prescreened candidates the credit bureaus use to supply your personal information to companies that want to issue you preapproved credit card offers through the mail. Your name will remain off those lists for two years.

You should also order your Social Security Earnings and Benefits Statement once a year to ensure that no one is committing Social Security fraud based on your Social Security number. You can obtain the forms required for requesting that information by calling the Social Security Administration automated line at 1-800-772-1213. Supply your name and address and the number of forms you want. This report is free.

The Privacy Rights Clearinghouse suggests you take several other steps to protect yourself:

- Have an unlisted phone number, or, at the least, don't include any professional designations in your listing, such as doctor or attorney, that would indicate affluence.
- Don't carry unnecessary identification with you, such as your Social Security card, birth certificate, or passport.
- Don't allow retailers to write your Social Security number on your checks.
- Be careful at bank ATM machines to ensure that no one obtains your personal identification number (PIN) by looking over your shoulder, and never throw ATM receipts in trash cans located near the machine.
- When creating PIN numbers, don't use the obvious, such as your birth date, address, or last four digits of your Social Security number.
- When you discard any type of personal information, rip it to shreds first. For maximum protection, use a cross-cut shredder.
- Never give your credit card number, bank account number,

or other personal numbers or identification to a stranger who calls, no matter what reason the person gives for needing it.

- Keep a list of your credit cards, the numbers, and expiration dates in a safe place in case the cards are stolen.
- When you use your credit cards, always check the amount charged on the receipt to be sure it's correct. Keep all your credit card receipts and reconcile them to your bill each month. Become familiar with the date the bill arrives each month, and if it's late, contact the issuer. If your card is stolen, report it immediately.

Some people swear that the most dangerous use of your credit card is for you to type its information into a Web site on the Internet to purchase products. The fear is that the Internet is not secure or protected and anyone can access the information. Others say using your credit card to purchase goods over the Internet is safer than giving your credit card number to someone you call on the phone to purchase a product, or to a waiter in a restaurant who disappears with the card for five minutes. The bottom line is that anyone who has access to your card can steal the number.

If you find you are the target of an identity fraud, the Privacy Rights Clearinghouse suggests you do the following:

- Alert the three credit bureaus listed above to place a fraud alert on your report, and ask for a copy of your credit report.
- Report the fraud to the police and provide as much documented evidence as you can. Ask to have a copy of the police report. You may need it to verify the crime when dealing with other vendors.
- Contact all creditors listed on your credit report. Close old credit card accounts if they've been affected, and open new ones with new account numbers.
- Call the post office, department of motor vehicles, the Social Security office, and your bank to be sure no one has changed your address, obtained a driver's license or Social Security card in your name, or accessed your bank account. If your checks have been stolen, close your account and open a new one. You may be asked to complete fraud affidavits if fraudulent accounts have been opened in your name at the bank or with the credit card companies.

- You may want to obtain a new driver's license if the old one has been used as identification by the imposter.
- Maintain good records of everything you do to resolve the problem.

You can obtain more information on this type of fraud from:

Privacy Rights Clearinghouse
1717 Kettner Avenue, Suite 105
San Diego, California 92101

619-298-3396

http://www.privacyrights.org

The Privacy Rights Clearinghouse's book *The Privacy Rights Handbook* can be purchased directly or at most major bookstores.

While the steps required to protect yourself from identity fraud may sound time-consuming and cumbersome, they're much less frustrating and devastating than trying to resolve the problem once it exists. Take the time and make the effort required to protect your identity. You're a unique, one-of-a-kind person. Make sure it stays that way.

Bronti Kelly, Temecula, California, Victim of Identity Theft

In May 1990 I was at a comedy club in Los Angeles with friends when I lost my wallet. All I had in it was my driver's license, Social Security card, active-duty air force military identification card, and four dollars. I filed a stolen wallet report with the Los Angeles Police Department.

In December 1990, I was selling electronic equipment at the May Department Store in Riverside, California. The manager called me in and said he was letting me go because he found out I had been apprehended for shoplifting on the previous June 2 at their L. A. Wilshire Boulevard store. I told them they were mistaken and was even able to prove it, so they let me stay. In January I was let go because I had been hired as a seasonal employee for the Christmas holidays. But when they let me go, they submitted that incorrect arrest information to a database maintained by their subsidiary which can be accessed by other employers for information about potential employees. Because of that incorrect information in that database, I was labeled a shoplifter, and I couldn't get a job anywhere.

With no income, I couldn't pay my bills. I eventually had to file Chapter 7 bankruptcy, and I lost my apartment. I took what possessions I could and started living in my car. When it broke down, I lived on the streets. In July 1994, after a year and a half of living in my car and on the streets, a bishop at a Catholic church in San Bernardino took me in. I eventually landed a job selling men's clothes at a department store. But on the day I was to start my training, they fired me. In a heated discussion, the employer commented that they didn't want criminals working for them. That comment made me think there was more of a problem than just the false shoplifting charge.

I went to the San Bernardino district attorney's office, and he checked my records. To my amazement, I had a police record ranging from arson to shoplifting to burglary to disturbing the peace to armed robbery. There was even an outstanding warrant for my arrest. That was in 1994, and that's the first time I realized all these problems were happening because someone had stolen my identity by stealing my wallet four years earlier. He was committing crimes in my name by giving the police my wallet every time he was arrested. His police record was the reason I couldn't get a job. He didn't destroy my credit and financial wherewithal directly by running up debt in my name, but he did destroy it indirectly in that I couldn't get a job to support myself. And the May Company perpetuated the problem by placing incorrect information in its database.

To this day I don't know who this guy is, but I have a mug shot of him from when he was arrested and used my name. He weighs about 180 pounds, has blond hair, brown eyes, and tattoos. I weigh about 130 pounds, have brown hair, blue eyes, wear glasses, and have no tattoos. I'm thirty-four years old, and because of him I've filed bankruptcy, I've been homeless, I can't get a full-time job, my credit is ruined, and my reputation has been tarnished.

I can't spend the rest of my life holding a grudge against this person. If I did that, I'd become eighty years old by the time I'm forty. Someday he'll be caught and he'll pay. In the meantime,

I'm working as a privacy rights activist and a spokesperson for victims of identity theft. I've also become an integral part of getting new laws passed that will make this type of crime more difficult to perpetrate in California in the future. I'd also like to create an organization that keeps tabs on databases to ensure that mistakes don't occur that can create a catastrophe in someone's life like what happened to me.

This has been a horrible experience, but one thing I've learned is that even though at one point I had lost everything, I never lost the ability to believe in myself. That's one thing no one can steal from you.

Checklist

Have you been:

- ❑ Refused credit due to large debts in your name that you never incurred?

- ❑ Getting calls from collection agencies regarding late payments on credit cards you don't own?

- ❑ Getting calls from your credit card company regarding out-of-character charges that you haven't made on your credit card?

- ❑ Neglecting to order copies of your credit report and Social Security Earnings and Benefits Statement on a regular basis?

- ❑ Including professional designations such as doctor or attorney in your phone listing?

- ❑ Carrying unnecessary identification with you, such as a Social Security card or passport?

- ❑ Allowing retailers to write your Social Security number on your checks?

- ❑ Using an obvious PIN and throwing away unshredded ATM slips or other documents?

- ❑ Giving out personal numbers such as credit card and bank account numbers to strangers on the phone?

❑   Neglecting to reconcile your credit card bill to your credit
       card receipts?

If you answered yes to any of these questions, you could already
be a victim of identity fraud and not know it.

CHAPTER 13

For a Fee, We'll Defraud You: Advance Fee Fraud

The only thing necessary for the triumph of evil is for good men to do nothing.

EDMUND BURKE, CONGRESSMAN

In May 1998, Janet Rockledge decided to combine all her debts by taking out a debt consolidation loan. She would use the money from the loan to pay off all her debts and then have just one payment per month. It was at that time that Rockledge saw an ad in the *Hutchinson News* that Northshore Financial was offering debt consolidation loans.

On May 20, 1998, she called the phone number in the ad and spoke to a company representative. During their conversation, the representative took Rockledge's application for a debt consolidation loan of ten thousand dollars. He said her loan request would be processed, and she would be contacted in a couple days.

A few days later, Rockledge received a call from the company representative, who said her loan had been approved and that he was faxing papers to her to sign. He also informed her that along with the signed application, she needed to fax to him a copy of her driver's license, Social Security card, and employment paycheck stubs. In addition, he explained that the terms of the loan required that she pay the first and last months' payments in advance by money order. The money order was to be in the amount of $895.46 and needed to be sent to him by express delivery before the loan could be released. On May 27, 1998, Rockledge purchased a money order and mailed it by registered mail.

When time passed and she didn't receive her loan, she called to find out the status of her application. The company representative told her that her loan had been placed with a private lender; however, he couldn't reveal the name of that lender. He told her to be patient and wait for the check to arrive. The check never arrived.

Rockledge reported the problem to the securities commissioner in her state, who investigated and found that neither Northshore Financial nor the company representative was registered as a loan broker in that state. The securities commissioner issued a cease-and-desist order against the company. That order helped to stop Northshore Financial from defrauding others in the state, but Rockledge lost her $895.46—money that she could have used to pay her debts.

What Rockledge experienced is called advance fee loan fraud, in which a supposed loan company offers to secure a loan for a borrower from a legitimate lending institution but first requires an up-front fee. The fee is typically a percentage of the gross loan amount. For instance, a loan of ten thousand dollars may carry a 5 percent fee, or five hundred dollars. After the fee is paid, the borrower never receives the loan, and the fee is gone. In reality, the company has no ability to make or obtain the loan.

There are two categories of advance fee loan fraud.

Business Advance Fee Loan Fraud

This category is aimed at small business owners, family businesses, and farmers. The loans are for large amounts, even in the millions of dollars, which generate fees of tens of thousands or hundreds of thousands of dollars per loan. The interest charged is always at below-market rates. This category of advance fee loan fraud was especially popular in the 1980s when interest rates were in the low-20-percent range and farmers were losing their farms and businesspeople were losing their businesses. It was extremely difficult to get credit, and even if an applicant did, it was at 17 or 18 percent.

The con artists would advertise in business and agricultural magazines that they had money available at 7 or 8 percent. The reason it was so cheap, the story went, was that they had access to overseas money from a Saudi oil prince or a Hong Kong business-man who wanted to move his money out of Hong Kong before the Chinese took over. It was a plausible story.

The con artist would ask the business owner or farmer for appraisals, income statements, and tax records. Then came the request for the up-front fee, which could be tens of thousands of dollars, depending on the size of the loan. After the fee was paid, the con artist would string the person along. The victim would be told that the money hadn't been sent yet because more time was needed for processing, or he needed to send more records. But vic-tims were always told not to worry—the money would be in their hands shortly. It never was.

Some con artists even try to convince their victims that if they apply for and receive a self-liquidating loan, they'll never have to pay the loan back. They're told that a portion of the principal of the loan will be used to purchase a zero coupon bond. When the bond matures, the money will be used to pay off the loan. The truth is that self-liquidating loans don't exist.

Individual Advance Fee Loan Fraud

The amount of money—both the loan and the fee—is for a much smaller amount in this type of advance fee loan fraud. The con artist targets individuals who are looking for debt consolidation loans, mortgage refinancing loans, or car loans in the amount of ten to twenty thousand dollars. The loans carry below-market inter-est rates and require an advance fee in the range of three to four hundred dollars or less. Typically the people the con artists seek out are those who have bad credit histories and can't get loans at banks, credit unions, or finance companies. Many of them target young people who are just starting out in their first job, have no credit history, and need money.

One con artist from South Carolina advertised on the Inter-net that consumers could get easy access to credit cards and loans with no credit check. All they had to do was send in forty-nine dollars. He bragged that he had an excellent record with the National Bureau of Consumer Affairs. The problem was that the National Bureau of Consumer Affairs was not a government agency, as its name implies. It was a company that the con artist himself owned and operated. The people who sent in forty-nine dollars didn't receive loans or credit cards. They received a list of companies that offered loans and credit cards based on credit checks.

Roadblocks to Prosecution

In both types of advance fee loan fraud, the victim is strung along after the fee is paid because the con artist wants to buy time. As soon as the victim knows she's been defrauded, the next phone call she'll make is to the authorities, and that means the con artist has to pull up stakes quickly and move on. But if the victim doesn't realize it's a con and can be convinced to keep sending more documents, the con artist has time to defraud others.

That extra time means a lot of money to these con artists. One con artist in Kansas City set up an office with a fax machine and a phone, made up a fancy name of Chase, Morgan, Stearns, and Lloyd, and put a business loan ad in the *New York Times*. Within just six months, he took in almost $500,000 in fees from fewer than ten victims.

Both business and individual advance fee loan fraud could be eradicated if potential victims understood that a legitimate lender does not ask for a fee to process a loan. In fact, the FTC's new Telemarketing Sales Rule makes it illegal for any telemarketer who promises consumers a loan or other credit to ask for money up front. Although there are legitimate fees associated with applying for a loan, such as a fee for a credit check or an appraisal, those amounts are fairly small and are often deducted out of the proceeds of the loan at the time of closing. Of course, some people with bad credit histories can't be approved for a loan from a legitimate lending institution. Although that can be a difficult situation, turning to an advance fee con artist is not the answer. Being robbed of what money you do have only makes matters worse.

It's difficult for the authorities to stop this con. There are federal laws against mail fraud and wire fraud, which these activities fall under, but at the federal level there's a shortage of resources, so other types of crime take priority. That means enforcement is left up to the states.

According to Larry Cook, director of the Enforcement Division of the Office of the Kansas Securities Commissioner, his office regularly responds to these bogus ads, not as the government but posing as potential borrowers. Once they have a reasonable belief that the con artist is violating the law, Cook's office issues a cease-and-desist order, an administrative order requiring the con artists to stop advertising and doing business in the state. Notification of that order is sent to a national computer database, where other states have access to the information.

If the con artists violate the cease-and-desist order and continue their fraud, the authorities can charge them criminally. But instead of violating the order and facing criminal charges, the con artists usually pick up shop and move to another state, setting up operations there. But to charge them criminally without first issuing the cease-and-desist order, the regulators would have to pay the advance fee and take the chance of losing the money. That approach is very time-consuming, requires a lot of manpower that isn't available, and can be very expensive.

Another problem the authorities face is that when it comes to individual advance fee fraud, approximately 90 percent of those scams are run out of Canada, where U.S. authorities have no jurisdiction. The state regulators have to go through the Justice Department to subpoena records and issue arrest warrants, a bureaucratic hassle.

While those are the two categories of advance fee loan fraud perpetrated from North America, another type of advance fee loan fraud comes from abroad.

The 419 Scam

A man in New York received a letter from an accountant in Nigeria who said that while he was conducting a corporate audit, he located almost twenty million dollars that was due to a now-defunct company. Although the company didn't exist anymore, the money did and would be paid to anyone who represented the defunct company. The Nigerian needed a foreign bank account where he could deposit the money. He told the New Yorker that if he'd allow him to deposit the money to his account for a short time, he'd pay him a commission of almost $6 million for his assistance.

During subsequent communications, the Nigerian told the New Yorker that to complete the transaction, he would have to go to Nigeria to sign papers. He also told him to bring an advance fee of almost $200,000 with him to cover certain expenses. When the New Yorker balked, the fee was reduced to $100,000. When he was still hesitant, the fee dropped to $75,000. The man didn't fall for the scam, and he escaped unscathed.

This is an example of what's called the Nigerian scam, or the 419 scam, named after the section of the Nigerian penal code that addresses fraud schemes. According to an article in the February 16, 1998, issue of *Barron's*, the Secret Service estimates that 419 schemes represent more than $100 million in fraud every year. During a six-month period in 1998, the JFK Mail Center in New York seized and destroyed more than two million of these letters. But others are slipping through. The Secret Service says its Financial Crimes Division receives approximately one hundred telephone calls and three hundred to five hundred pieces of related correspondence per day from victims. Potential victims in more than seventy-five countries have received these 419 scam letters. It has been estimated that the 419 scam is the third largest industry in Nigeria.

The scam is conducted in various ways, but the most prevalent is that an individual or company will receive a letter from an official of a foreign government or agency offering to transfer millions of dollars into the person's or company's bank account. The reason is typically that the government overpaid on some procurement contract and the official doesn't want to return the money to the government. Instead, he wants to get it out of the country. The victim is asked to provide blank company letterheads, bank account information, and phone and fax numbers. To make the scam look legitimate, the con artist sends the victim numerous documents that contain official-looking seals, stamps, and logos. Eventually the victim is encouraged to travel to the foreign country and pay large advance fees for various taxes, attorney fees, transaction fees, or even bribes. If the victim pays the fee, there are always other problems that crop up while completing the transaction that require the victim to pay even more fees.

Victims who have pursued this "opportunity" and agreed to travel to Nigeria to complete paperwork and pay an advance fee have been told they don't need a visa to enter Nigeria. In fact, it's a serious offense in Nigeria to enter without a valid visa. When the victim arrives without a visa, the con artist bribes the Nigerian officials to allow the person to enter the country. His illegal entry is then used to threaten him to release more funds. And these con artists aren't nervous about using physical force. In June 1995, an American was murdered in Lagos, Nigeria, while pursuing one of these scams. Other foreign nationals have been reported missing. European con artists, who also target victims in the United States and other countries, have recently adopted the 419 scam.

Other Types of Scams

Other types of advance fee scams also exist. In August 1998, five people were arrested in Florida for running an advance fee job service scam. They were charged with mail fraud, wire fraud, and money laundering. They advertised job openings in newspapers nationwide, but when applicants called, they were urged to pay an advance fee by credit card and were promised a refund if they weren't satisfied. The problem was that the advertised jobs didn't exist. When the applicants called to complain because there was no response from the company after the fee was paid, they were put off with excuses until the company finally ceased to exist.

Another type of advance fee scam involves scholarships. These con artists claim to have access to scholarships that college-bound students wouldn't be able to locate on their own. For a fee, they guarantee they can obtain a scholarship for any student. If, for some reason, a scholarship isn't located, they promise, the up-front fee will be refunded. The truth is that there are no scholarships, and the fees are never refunded. The National Association of Student Financial Aid Administrators estimates that 350,000 students lose $5 million to these scams each year.

Protecting Yourself From Advance Fee Scams

Whether you get an offer from Nigeria, Europe, Canada, or right here at home that requires any type of advance fee, don't bite; you'll only lose. Although the offers these people make may sound plausible, ask yourself why an unknown lender from another state or country would be more willing to provide you with a loan than your own local financial institution.

If, despite warnings, you accept any type of offer that requires an advance fee, check out the person and the company with your state regulators. Ask why you're told to supply money up front. Ask for names of other customers the company has worked with and, with a bit of cynicism, call those people and ask if they were satisfied. Call the state authorities or the Better Business Bureau to find out if the person has a valid license for engaging in lending or other activities. If you're applying for a loan, insist on knowing the name of the lending institution that is supposed to fund the loan. Call the lender, and verify that all the information you have as to the terms of the loan is correct. If the source of funds is a foreign investor or an offshore bank you can't contact, that's a sure sign of trouble.

If you need money and a bank isn't willing to talk to you, try to borrow the money from a friend or a relative. Better yet, begin a savings program that will allow you to save the money you need yourself. Most important, start repairing your damaged credit rating so that in the future, a legitimate lending institution will be happy to work with you. If you don't know how to do that, find a counselor or trusted adviser who can guide you in making the right decisions for your situation. It's the only safe way to do business.

Barbara Morton, Vice President of Housing and Education, Consumer Credit Counseling Service of Central Florida, Orlando, Florida

Often people get into debt and get so overwhelmed they don't know what to do. They need to know that there is help available. A consumer credit counseling agency can help them determine their options and create a plan that will get them back in good standing. They can find accredited, nonprofit agencies by calling their local United Way office or the National Foundation for Consumer Credit at 1-800-388-2227. Both organizations are nonprofit and charge clients no fee or a small fee, unlike some for-profit agencies that charge clients a percentage of their total debt just to give them advice.

Our counselors make a professional, impartial assessment of clients' debts, income, expenses, and assets and make recommendations. We work with their creditors to stretch out payments, waive interest, stop late charges, and possibly even bring the account current. Most creditors allow us a good deal of flexibility and are willing to work with us. Some clients have enough money, but they're just mismanaging it. Others have an income that may be just a little short to cover their bills, and finding a part-time job of just ten hours a month will make the difference. Sometimes we recommend that clients sell their homes and purchase a less expensive home or even rent for a short time. The Federal Housing Administration has a pre-foreclosure sale program that's designed to help people sell their houses quickly. The Veterans Administration also has a short sale program in which people can sell their homes rather than face foreclosure.

There are some options we don't necessarily recommend, such as a 125 percent mortgage, a consolidation loan, or bankruptcy. A 125 percent mortgage just adds more debt and makes it even more difficult to get back on track. And once the clients have a 125 percent mortgage, they can't sell their house. Consolidation loans don't work for most people either. You can't borrow your way out of debt. When people take out consolidation loans, they tend to keep their credit cards and start maxing them out again and end up deeper in debt. And bankruptcy, which stays on credit reports for ten years, isn't a good option because it doesn't cure certain debts such as federal tax payments, student loans, child support, or mortgage payments.

If you're in debt and having credit problems, never pay a fee to obtain a loan. Instead, find an accredited, nonprofit credit-counseling agency and get some professional advice. It's definitely worth an hour of your time.

Checklist

Have you been:

❑ Offered a self-liquidating loan?

❑ Offered a loan in which you must pay an advance fee prior to receiving the loan proceeds?

❑ Offered a loan at below-market interest rates?

❑ Offered easy access to credit cards with no credit check required?

❑ Offered a loan through a cold call that originated in Canada?

❑ Offered a commission by someone in a foreign country if you allow him to deposit money in your bank account?

❑ Offered access to job opportunities in return for paying an advance fee?

❑ Offered access to college scholarships if you pay an advance fee?

If you answered yes to any of these questions, you may be the target of an advance fee scheme.

CHAPTER 14

Miscellaneous Frauds at Home and Around the World

Experience is that marvelous thing that enables you to recognize a mistake when you make it again.

F. P. JONES

Who wouldn't want to be a crime fighter helping to eradicate crime from our society? Well, we can't all be Batman, but every once in a while, we may get the opportunity to help catch the bad guy. For instance, you may get a call from someone claiming to be a bank examiner at the bank where you have your account. The examiner tells you he suspects that a teller working at the bank is dishonest. He asks you to help expose this person by going to the bank and making a cash withdrawal of one thousand dollars. The examiner wants to see if the teller alters the bank records to show you've made a withdrawal of two thousand dollars and then pockets the extra one thousand dollars. After you make the withdrawal, you're to meet the bank examiner at a predetermined location and give him the money and the withdrawal receipt, which he'll use as evidence when he audits the transaction. He promises that the money will be credited back to your account. When the teller's misdeeds are exposed, you can say you were part of the team that helped do it! Maybe you are Batman!

What you are is Batman gone awry. Unfortunately the person who called you is not a bank examiner, there is no dishonest teller at the bank, and the person you turned your money over to is not going to credit it back into your account. It's called the bank examiner scam, and it's just one more fraud that con artists use to steal your money.

Although this book covers most of the major types of fraud that everyone should be aware of, it is by no means all-inclusive. If it were, only Arnold Schwarzenegger would be strong enough to pick it up. This chapter briefly covers other popular types of fraud con artists perpetrate against unsuspecting victims.

At Your Door

The $12.95 Brick

Most people are willing to help out a friend or neighbor, which is what con artists count on. If a delivery person arrived on your doorstep with a package addressed to your neighbor and explained that your neighbor wasn't home, would you accept it? Would you pay the $12.95 C.O.D. charge knowing your neighbor would appreciate it and pay you back? If you didn't, your neighbor would have to go to the post office on Saturday and stand in line forever to retrieve the package. We all know how frustrating that is.

If you accept the package and pay the charge, however, when your neighbor opens it, you may discover that you paid $12.95 for a worthless brick. Goodbye $12.95!

Magazine Subscriptions

Another knock on your door! This time the person is selling magazine subscriptions—not so sinister, right? The problem is that you'll pay a higher price for these magazine subscriptions than if you went to the newsstand and bought them. Or the person may claim to be doing a survey on reading habits or offer you free or prepaid subscriptions. You'll probably end up buying multiple subscriptions without even realizing what you've done.

Social Security Fraud

If you need a revised Social Security card because you've lost yours or you had a name change, the Social Security Administration will send you one for free. If you need a Social Security number for a child, you can get one for free. If you want a copy of your personal Earnings and Benefit Estimate Statement that shows how much you've paid in and how much you'll collect at retirement, the Social Security Administration will send you one for free.

Con artists offer all these services for a fee to victims who don't realize they can obtain these services at no cost. Other con artists have even threatened victims with the possibility of losing their Social Security benefits unless they send a contribution or membership fee.

If you receive a fraudulent solicitation for Social Security services, complain to the Better Business Bureau or your state's attorney general. Also, give the complete mailing to your local postmaster, or send it to:

Social Security Administration
Office of the Inspector General
6401 Security Boulevard, Room 300, Altmeyer Building
Baltimore, Maryland 20260-2100

Postal Fraud

This fraud is perpetrated by the lowest of the low. These con artists scan obituaries to find the recently widowed who are mourning the loss of their spouse. They send the widow overpriced merchandise that they claim was ordered by the deceased spouse, or they simply send authentic-looking bills claiming the spouse had received the merchandise prior to dying. Many times the grieving widow will accept the merchandise and pay the bill, or simply pay a bill without proof of a purchase.

On the Street

ATM Cons

You're out shopping and realize you're short on cash, so you stop at an ATM. Just as you enter your personal identification number (PIN) into the machine, a maintenance person approaches and says she has to do some work on the machine so you'll need to use the other ATM. You use the other machine, get your money, and leave. Meanwhile, the "maintenance person" has your PIN and starts withdrawing money. Con artists have also been known to pose as maintenance people asking victims for their PIN so they can "test" the machine. Also be aware of anyone standing in line behind you so close that he or she can determine what your PIN is as you enter it.

Credit Card Frauds

You go to the store and buy a new coat for $115, but when you sign the credit card slip, you don't even notice that the clerk imprinted a $175 charge. Or maybe the clerk takes your credit card in the back room and imprints two vouchers: one for you to sign and one for her to forge your name to later. Or maybe the clerk copies down your credit card number from the carbon paper and uses it later to make purchases by mail or phone.

Payment Packing

Did you ever buy a car and finance it through the dealership? If so, you may have been a victim of payment packing, in which a dealer sells you additional services or products without your knowledge. Let's say you buy a car, and the dealer tells you that your monthly payments will be $300 per month. The monthly payment that covers the cost of the car and interest may calculate out to $270, but the dealer throws in a service contract, credit insurance, security devices, or chemical protection products without informing you and charges you an extra $30 per month. Without realizing it, you've bought products or services you didn't want, and you're probably paying a higher rate of interest for the loan than your local financial institution would have charged.

Investing Abroad

It seems as if the big hitters always get all the good investments. You're just a little guy trying to get a good return on your money. But then you find an investment promoter who tells you that you can invest like the big guys. All you have to do is give him your money, he'll pool it with money he collects from other small investors, and in conjunction with a large offshore bank he'll use the money to buy international bank notes that offer huge returns like the big investors collect. The details of exactly how the investment works aren't available, but it's your chance to get into investments that were never open to you before.

If you invest, you'll wish this investment still wasn't open to you, because you've just lost your money.

So maybe international bank notes are a little exotic and difficult to understand. But certificates of deposit (CDs) are pretty vanilla-type investments. One con artist promised investors 30 to 40 percent returns on CDs and other investments through a bank in the Marshall Islands. Unfortunately, the bank, which existed only on paper, had only one employee: a gas station attendant in the Marshall Islands who went to the post office each day, picked up investors' checks, and mailed them to the con artist in Washington State. About four hundred investors lost seven million dollars in this swindle.

From the Heart

When Minnesotans were solicited by the American Federation of Police (AFP) for donations, they were told that for thirty years, the charity had been providing critical support to families of police officers killed in action. In reality, the AFP had been in business for seventeen years, and most families of slain officers had never heard of it. That's because only two cents of every dollar actually made it to the Police Family Survivors Fund.

Every year Americans dole out $130 billion to more than 300,000 charities—most honest, a few bogus. Following are several tips to help you ensure that you're giving to a charity that will use your money for the purpose intended:

- *Know the charity.* Don't be fooled by sound-alike charity names. Ask for written information, such as a recent annual report. Ask where the money goes. At least 60 percent or more should go toward program services, and the remaining 40 percent or less to administrative and fund-raising costs.
- *Don't respond to pressure.* If you're not familiar with the charity and don't want to donate, say no despite the charity's pressure to donate immediately.

- *Keep records.* Never give cash or your credit card number to a solicitor. Pay by check or money order and obtain a receipt for any donations of $250 or more.
- *Understand that "tax exempt" doesn't always mean "tax deductible."* Not all charities are eligible to receive tax-deductible contributions. Tax exempt means the organization pays no taxes, whereas tax deductible means the donor can deduct contributions on his or her federal tax return.
- *Find out whom you're talking to. Is it a volunteer, a charity employee, or a professional fund-raiser?* Professional fund-raisers charge such high fees that the charity may receive as little as 20 percent of what's collected.
- *Don't fall prey to emotional appeals.* The sob story or hard-luck tale is geared to work on your emotions. Be sure you know the real story of how the money will be used.
- *Beware of gift offers.* Free key rings, address labels, calendars, and greeting cards mean higher fund-raising costs and less money that goes to support the charity's cause. If you keep the gift, you are not required to make a contribution. In fact, it's illegal for a charity to demand payment for unordered merchandise.

Check out national charities by contacting:
  - National Charities Information Bureau: phone: 1-212-929-6300; e-mail: ncib@bway.net; Web site: www.give.org
  - American Institute of Philanthropy: phone: 1-301-913-5200; Web site: www.charitywatch.org
  - Philanthropic Advisory Service, Council of Better Business Bureaus: phone: 1-703-276-0100; Web site: www.bbb.org

To check out local or regional charities, call the local Better Business Bureau or the local United Way office and ask if the organization supports that specific charity.

Once you've determined that a charity is worthwhile and accountable, give generously. Many charities provide valuable services and depend on contributions to stay afloat.

Protecting Yourself

You can protect yourself from these frauds by adhering to these simple rules:

- Never believe that a bank official would ask a customer to help expose a dishonest employee.
- Never accept a C.O.D. for someone unless the person has specifically asked you to.
- Never order magazine subscriptions except through the magazine itself.
- Never believe that you have to pay someone to assist you in obtaining Social Security services. Those services are always free.
- Never pay for merchandise sent to you that you didn't order, or for which you can't obtain proof of purchase.
- Never give your ATM card to a repairman or assist in testing the ATM; memorize your PIN rather than writing it down; always complete any ATM action you begin; and always block the vision of anyone around you when entering your PIN.
- Never sign a credit card slip without checking the amount charged; destroy all carbons and keep copies of receipts to reconcile to your monthly bill; and always report missing or stolen cards immediately.
- Never finance a car through the dealership without first checking out the financing through a bank or credit union, and always focus on negotiating trade-in, price, interest rate, and terms so you understand exactly what your monthly payment includes.
- Never put money in offshore or international investments without checking them out thoroughly and making sure you understand exactly what they are and how they work.
- Never donate to a charity without reaching the charity, asking the questions listed earlier, and ensuring that your money will indeed help the cause you want to support.

It's up to you to protect yourself from these swindlers. By following these rules, you'll be able to stop them in their tracks.

Jane Kusic, Founder and President, White Collar Crime 101, McLean, Virginia

My husband is a real estate and corporate lawyer, and in the 1980s he had a client whom we became so friendly with that my husband and I vacationed with him and his wife, our children visited each other, and I even went to work for him. We trusted him implicitly. By 1986, he owed my husband a half-million dollars in legal fees, we had lent him money, we had co-signed notes with him, and we had invested with him. That's when we found out he was a con artist. We lost more than a million dollars to him. We subsequently found out that he had conned hundreds of people, financial institutions, and businesses out of more than $104 million. He had stashed most of the money in banks in the Caribbean and Europe. None of it was recovered, and no one got any money back.

When you first realize you've been defrauded, you go numb, and you don't want to believe it. You tell yourself it's a mistake, and the con artist is going to give you your money back. You keep that hope because without hope, you have nothing. At the same time you feel stupid, embarrassed, and angry. You contact law enforcement, but they typically can't help you. So you contact an attorney, but the attorney wants a retainer to take your case, and you don't have any money left. Society loves a winner, and in a fraud case, the con man is the winner and the victim is the loser. Your friends ask how you could have fallen for such a scam, and they assure you they'd be too smart for that to happen to them. Finally, depression sets in. Over the years, I've even seen victims attempt and commit suicide.

After we were defrauded, I had to find answers, so I did extensive research and thought a lot about what had happened. I even went to the FBI. I found that because fraud is not a violent crime, people don't become outraged. No one ever considered creating any formal support programs or organizations like rape crises centers for rape victims or Mothers Against Drunk Drivers for those who have lost loved ones to auto accidents caused by alcohol. That's when I decided that I would create an organization that would help educate people on how to avoid fraud and offer emotional support to fraud victims. I started White Collar Crime 101.

People can call our organization at 1-800-440-2261 and order literature on fraud prevention and victimization. Over the years, I've talked to thousands of victims, and they're happy just to have someone to talk to who understands and listens. I let victims know that they're not stupid and that people of all ages and socioeconomic strata are scammed. I encourage them to talk to other victims. I assure them that it's not their fault; they're the victim.

White-collar crime is a game of manipulation and mind control. It's like a psychological rape. Victims need a place to turn for support and advice. There are victim specialists working hard to organize formal programs for fraud victims. I hope this will become a reality soon.

Checklist

Have you been:

- ❏ Asked by a bank examiner to help expose a dishonest bank employee?
- ❏ Asked by a delivery service person to sign and pay for a C.O.D. package for a neighbor?
- ❏ Asked to purchase magazine subscriptions or to complete a survey by someone who comes to your door?
- ❏ Solicited for Social Security services for a fee?
- ❏ Sent a bill for merchandise you never received?
- ❏ Asked by a maintenance person to help test an ATM?
- ❏ Encouraged to finance a vehicle purchase through an automobile dealership without being given a complete breakdown of what's included in the monthly payments?
- ❏ Offered an investment that involves offshore banking in which the details of how the investment works are vague or unavailable?
- ❏ Offered an investment in international CDs that pay extraordinarily high rates of return?

❑ Encouraged to donate money to a charity that you're not familiar with, is unwilling to provide financial information to you, and offers free trinkets to entice you to give?

If you answered yes to any of these questions, you may be the targeted victim of a fraudulent scheme.

PART SEVEN

THE TOOLS OF FRAUD

CHAPTER 15

The Call That Can Cost You Your Nest Egg: Telemarketing Fraud

A verbal contract isn't worth the paper it's written on.

SAMUEL GOLDWYN, FILM PRODUCER

Broker: . . . I have clients that have been with me for five or six years now. My commissions are made off of them. I don't need little guys like you to make money off of. I build guys like you up to be hundred-, two-hundred-thousand-, quarter-million-dollar accounts in six to seven months. I know in two to three years when you have a seven figure portfolio over here, all the problems you are going to have with me, . . . today is that you didn't know me three years ago and you didn't step in and buy five thousand shares. Now . . . stop jerking your chain and my chain and let's get this account open and get the ball rolling.

Victim: Let's send the information to me and let me review it, and let's make a phone call.

Broker: . . . Let me say this to you . . . if you had a, if you had a 3 thousand dollars, that showed you 2 thousand dollars in profit in the next 45 days, I have a feeling you're going to send me 10 to 15 on my next one. And the information I send you, believe me it's, when you see it all in black and white in the Federal Express package and you're looking at it all spread out on your desk and you see every single piece of information I told you was fact, then you're going to be comfortable.

Victim: So you're going to send me the information?

Broker: I want to send the information, but what I want to do is this. I want to get you a confirmation of you owning Inso. Anything under 11 dollars a share is a steal.

Victim: You're gonna send me the information, then you're gonna call me back. Right?

Broker: I want you to get involved with this stock today so when I can tell you that my timing and pricing is everything and not just bull . . .

Victim: I, okay, I uh, I'll give you a hint, if I have to buy it tomorrow at 12 bucks a share, I won't blame you.

Broker: Well, . . . I don't care if you blame me. My job is very, very simple. I am to buy you stocks when the timing is right, not on your timing and pricing because if you want to buy stocks on your timing and pricing you're going to make 10, 12 percent like every other investor out there. Every investor in America looks for guys like me that can buy stocks two to three weeks before Wall Street has the attention on it and before the stock is up 13, 14 percent. Now you add 13, 14 percent on top of the 30, 40 percent that we're already making on it, that's how real Wall Street brokers work. I'm notgonna buy stocks when you're ready. I buy stocks when I'm ready.

This is an excerpt of a telemarketing call made on July 10, 1997, by a New York scam artist. This call, as well as numerous others, provided one of the centerpieces of the New York attorney general's public hearings on micro-cap stock fraud during the summer of 1997. Pretty intimidating for the victim, don't you think? Well, it would be except that the broker didn't know he was talking to a securities regulator who was sitting in his office at the Securities Division of Utah.

Common Scams

The telephone has been a popular tool for con artists to communicate their frauds to their victims for decades. Telemarketing schemes involve all kinds of scams, many of which we've examined in other chapters: micro-cap stocks, commodities, prizes, Ponzis and pyramids, magazine sales, high-tech frauds, and more. The National Fraud Information Center (NFIC) says that no one really knows how much money is lost to telemarketing fraud, but it estimates that it's in the billions of dollars per year. The NFIC identified the following as the top ten telemarketing frauds in 1998:

1. *Telephone cramming.* This is when companies add charges to your telephone bill for optional services you never authorized, such as voice mail, paging, a personal 800 number or club memberships that bill through the phone company.
2. *Advance fee loans.* These are promises of personal or business loans that require the payment of fees in advance. (They are covered thoroughly in Chapter 13.)
3. *Slamming.* During this phone call, you'll be tricked into changing your phone service to another carrier without even realizing you've done it.
4. *Prizes and sweepstakes.* This is basically a "you've won a prize [car, money, boat], send me money if you want it" scam. If you send money or let the caller charge your credit card, you may never hear from him again. If you do hear from the person, the prize won't be anywhere near the value of the money you paid.
5. *Work-at-home plans.* This is your opportunity to stuff envelopes, type letters, fabricate jewelry, or a hundred other activities you can do at home and make tons of money. Don't believe it.
6. *Magazine sales.* By the time you're done dealing with this per-

son, you've bought hundreds of dollars of magazines you don't want and that you could have bought on the newsstand for much less.

7. *Credit card offers.* If you have a bad credit history, you may get a call from a telemarketer who will gladly issue you a credit card if you pay a fee in advance. Trust me; the card will never reach you.

8. *Pay-per-call services.* In this scam, *you* call the con artist. He advertises in a reputable publication or sends you a postcard that provides you with a 900 number you can call to access information or entertainment services. Or maybe the postcard says you've won a guaranteed prize. You just have to call a 900 number to claim it. When you call, you're enticed into paying a fee so you can be awarded a "better" prize than the one you initially won. Of course, there are no prizes. Even worse, when you get your phone bill after calling the 900 number, you'll find that these calls can cost you as much as fifty dollars each!

9. *Business opportunities and franchises.* As we saw in Chapter 10, these scams involve exaggerated claims of potential profits through investments in various business opportunities or franchises.

10. *Travel and vacations.* The vacation is free, but you are told that you have to send in money to cover certain fees, or you may be convinced to send in money for upgrades. After you pay your money, you never hear from these people again. Or you may actually be awarded a free vacation. You'll find, however, that when you try to schedule it, space won't be available at the time you want, or there'll be some other problem with the accommodations. The vacation will be virtually impossible to schedule. If you are able to schedule it, you'll find that the only part that's free is the hotel room. You have to pay your own way to the destination, then pay taxes and service fees upon arrival. To check to see if complaints have been lodged against a travel agent, call the American Society of Travel Agents (ASTA) Consumer Affairs Department, at 1-703-739-8739, or check its Web site at www.astanet.com.

Although these frauds remain popular, con artists are always developing new types of telemarketing fraud. One that has become prevalent is called cramming. Cramming involves bogus charges that show up on a person's phone bill for services the person never agreed to purchase, such as voice mail paging, personal 800 numbers, or even non-phone-related services such as charges for club memberships that bill via the phone company.

How the Scam Works

One of the reasons telemarketing fraud is so prevalent is that a telemarketing operation is cheap to run. All a con artist needs is a big room with a bank of phones and a bunch of people to make phone calls. In the 1920s these operations were coined "boiler rooms." Customers never go to the telemarketers' offices, so they rent the cheapest space available in a building—often the boiler room. It's also called that because the operators "turn up the heat" on their potential victims.

Boiler room operators typically call people in cities and states other than where the telemarketer is located because that makes it more difficult for local, state, and federal prosecution, which often requires victims to be in the immediate vicinity. Large numbers of telemarketers now set up shop in Canada and target Americans as their victims, making it even more difficult for authorities to find them. When authorities do discover the fraud, the telemarketers close up shop and move to another location, making apprehension and prosecution nearly impossible.

Fraudulent telemarketers target anyone with a phone—often senior citizens because they're home during the day. These con artists even scan newspaper obituaries looking for widows and widowers who may be about to collect lump-sum life insurance payments. One woman in Florida received a call from a cemetery plot salesman right after her husband died and purchased a plot, where she placed her husband's ashes. The salesman called again and talked her into buying another adornment to the grave. By the time she had completed four phone conversations with this person, she had purchased a mausoleum, statues, and benches, for a total cost of $150,000.

Fraudulent telemarketers also target small business owners, whose phone numbers they obtain from Dun & Bradstreet survey lists. They also use phone directories to obtain names and phone numbers, or they may purchase lists from other con artists, paying as much as a dollar for each name. If you've fallen victim to one of these scams before, your name may be on what's called a *sucker list* or a *mooch list* and may sell for as much as twenty-five dollars. If that's the case, the con artist may already have a lot of information about you, including your age, income, health status, hobbies, occupation, marital status, education, and even what magazines you read. You may receive a reload call—a call from someone who, for a fee, says he wants to help you recover the money you lost in a previous fraud. It's just another scam.

If the telemarketer is trying to sell you an investment and tells you he has been in the business for twenty years and never before saw such a good opportunity, don't believe it. He may be a twenty-two-year-old who has never worked in the investment business a day in his life. He's simply reading from a script that's been meticulously written to include convincing rebuttals to every objection anyone can have. If you stand your ground, he may question your intelligence or your ability to make a decision. Fraudulent telemarketers can be very aggressive because their pay is often determined by how many victims they defraud. The telemarketer in a boiler room who cons the most victims in a day may even get a bonus.

Some telemarketers call their victims once and use extremely high-pressure sales tactics, saying that there are "only a few left" or the offer is "about to expire." Others may call several times over the span of several weeks or a few months and be extremely friendly and kind. The first call will ply you with background information on an investment as the caller tries to earn your trust. During the second call, he'll tempt you with information about a big deal that is about to happen. On the third call, he'll move in for the kill.

Some telemarketers use voice switching, in which he says his boss wants to talk to you for a moment. The boss (really the same person disguising his voice) will come on the line and tell you how exciting this offer is and congratulate you on your good luck. When talking to a telemarketer who's offering you a fraudulent investment, you may even hear the sounds of the hustle and bustle of a large Wall Street brokerage firm emanating from the background. Those are sound effects coming from a tape recorder.

Most telemarketers demand that you make an immediate decision; they won't give you their address, and they'll try to avoid using the mail at all costs so they can avoid facing mail fraud charges if caught. They won't honor your request for written information because whatever they're selling is a new offer, they explain, and the written marketing material isn't ready yet, or there simply isn't time to send it. When you hear the words "trust me," it's time to hang up the phone. There's one other trait that all fraudulent telemarketers possess: As soon as you realize you've made a mistake and you want to talk to them, they'll be gone. They can disappear overnight.

Protecting Yourself From Telemarketers

Regulators are trying to stop fraudulent telemarketers. In 1995 the FTC adopted the Telemarketing Sales Rule, which sets forth the following requirements that telemarketers must follow:
- Give potential customers key information that would affect their investment and purchasing decisions.
- Promptly disclose that the call is a sales call.
- Explain the nature and total cost of goods or services being sold.
- Explain the risk, liquidity, earnings potential, or profitability of any investment offered.
- Restrict their calls to the hours between 8:00 A.M. and 9:00 P.M. your local time.
- Cease calling you subsequently to your request not to phone again. You can ask the telemarketer to place your name on a "do not call" list.

As a consumer, you are also protected against unfair and deceptive trade practices by the Federal Trade Commission Act. You have the following rights:
- To request written information about products or services, including any promised guarantees or refunds.
- To require the company to ship your ordered merchandise to you within the promised time frame. If no specific time frame was promised, your order should be shipped within thirty days.

- To dispute a charge on your credit card and withhold payment if an order isn't delivered as promised, until the problem is investigated. You are required, however, to notify your credit card company of a disputed charge within sixty days after the first bill containing the error is mailed to you.

Telemarketing has gotten a bad reputation because of the con artists who use it as a tool to steal money. But by no means is all telemarketing fraudulent. Many legitimate goods and services are sold through telemarketing by honest people who are working to make a legitimate living. If you're going to do business with a telemarketer, it's your job to ask questions and try to determine if the person you're talking to is legitimate or fraudulent.

- Always ask for the person's name and the company name, address, and phone number. Then ask how the company got your name.
- Ask what governmental agencies regulate this business and who the company is required to register with.
- Insist on receiving written information on a product or service that includes exactly what it is, how it works, what the total cost will be, what the refund policies are, and what other recourse you have if you're not satisfied.
- Don't let the person pressure you into a quick decision. Take the time to check the company out with the Better Business Bureau, your attorney general's office, or other consumer agencies.
- Never give out credit card numbers, bank account numbers, or other personal information to someone you don't know.

If the person on the other end of the phone line is a legitimate telemarketer, she'll answer your questions completely and not try to intimidate you.

If you find you've become the victim of a telemarketing scam, report it to your state's attorney general, the Better Business Bureau, or the Office of Consumer Protection immediately. You should also call the NFIC at 1-800-876-7060 and report it. Your call will be logged in to a computerized national law enforcement database that the Federal Trade Commission, FBI, Secret Service, U.S. Postal Inspection Service, Department of Justice, and other telemarketing fraud-fighting agencies use.

If you have trouble hanging up on someone or saying no, you might want to consider using your answering machine to screen calls. If the person leaving a message is someone you don't know, don't pick up. After leaving a couple of messages, the telemarketer will move on to someone he can reach and leave you alone.

The authorities are endeavoring to reduce the amount of telemarketing fraud that exists, but we, as potential victims, have to help. Every time your phone rings, be aware that the person at the other end of the line may be sitting in a room full of other crooks, liars, and cheats who make their living by stealing your hard-earned money. Help the authorities by hanging up the phone. You'll be richer for it.

Timothy J. Healy, Supervisory Special Agent and Program Manager for Telemarketing Fraud, Federal Bureau of Investigation, Washington, D.C.

Our most recent initiative against telemarketing fraud began with Operation Disconnect, a three-phase operation focusing on telemarketers who offer prizes and gifts for money. In phase one, undercover FBI agents convinced telemarketers that we could give them access to the services of a machine that didn't really exist. It was an automatic dialer that could dial one thousand local people per hour and pass along the telemarketer's message to them. For example, if the telemarketer was in Atlanta, we'd say we had a machine in Chicago that would dial local numbers, give the people the telemarketer's message, and tell them to call the telemarketer if they wanted to claim their prize. We said we had machines all over the country and could inundate their boiler rooms with incoming calls. The telemarketers jumped at the "service" because it saved them from having to buy lists of people to call and from having to make long-distance phone calls.

Phase two was to interview the telemarketers to determine what message they wanted on the automatic dialer to convince people to call them. After they bought our "service," they allowed us to interview their employees, who told us how they operate, basically confessing about how they defraud people.

Phase three was the hot test. We told them we were going to turn the dialer on for fifteen minutes. We said the dialer could contact 250 people in fifteen minutes, and of those, about 100 would answer the phone, and of those, about 20 would be convinced to make the call. When we told them the dialer was on, we had undercover agents start calling the telemarketer. They never knew we were the FBI, and we taped them trying to defraud our agents.

In all, 400 people were convicted. On average, each person was sentenced to about twenty-seven months in jail, with the owners getting more time and the lower-level employees getting less. In San Diego, there were probably one hundred fraudulent phone rooms before Operation Disconnect, and now there are virtually none. Salt Lake City had about sixty-five, and they're also shut down.

After Operation Disconnect, in conjunction with other governmental and nongovernmental agencies, we launched Operation Senior Sentinel, in which senior citizens targeted by fraudulent telemarketers allowed us to take control of their phone lines. When the telemarketers called those lines, we took the calls and taped the con artists running their scams. We cataloged those tapes and set up a National Tape Library; anyone doing an investigation on a telemarketer can contact the library to see if there's a tape that'll help the case. To date, more than twelve thousand tape recordings of illegal solicitations have been compiled, providing law enforcement with invaluable information as to the con artists' method of operation and means of avoiding detection and prosecution.

On December 17, 1998, through a coordinated effort among the FBI, thirty-five state attorneys general, and federal prosecutors, we announced the arrest of 926 subjects through Operation Double Barrel. In Operation Double Barrel, undercover agents and FBI-trained senior citizens posed as individuals who were previously defrauded. Through phone conversations with fraudulent telemarketers, they gathered evidence for possible legal action.

In Operation Disconnect, I talked to more than five hundred telemarketers undercover, and I can tell you from this experience that telemarketing is one crime you can fix if you address it. Telemarketers make a conscious decision to defraud people. If we continue to investigate them and prosecute them vigorously, we can provide a deterrent that'll make them decide it's not worth it.

The FBI is also involved in consumer awareness. In conjunction with the American Association of Retired Persons, we've set up reverse boiler rooms. When we go in with a search warrant to arrest these telemarketers, we confiscate their victim lists. We then call those victims and warn them that they're on these lists and that they need to be careful when they get these types of calls.

Fraudulent telemarketing could be eradicated if people would just follow three rules when they get these calls: (1) If it sounds too good to be true, it's probably a fraud; (2) If they ask for money up front, it's a fraud; (3) If you do a little research before you send in money for whatever reason, you'll probably find it's a fraud. If you do become a victim of a fraudulent telemarketer, contact the FBI, the Better Business Bureau, and your state law enforcement agencies. Call as many authorities as you can.

It's our job to put people who commit federal crimes in jail, and I think we do that fairly well. But if the public protects itself by following the three rules and all the law enforcement agencies continue to investigate and prosecute these people, we should be able to reduce telemarketing fraud substantially. We just need to work together.

Checklist

Have you been:

❑ Receiving phone calls in which the caller offers you prizes, work-at-home plans, credit cards, magazine subscriptions, vacations, or other types of offers?

❑ Receiving phone calls in which the caller offers you a can't-lose, risk-free investment?

❑ Receiving phone calls in which the caller uses extreme pressure or harassment to force you into purchasing an item or making an investment?

❏   Receiving phone calls in which the caller offers to send a
    courier to your home to pick up a check?

❏   Receiving phone calls in which the caller doesn't disclose that
    it's a sales call, doesn't explain the nature or cost of what's
    being sold, continues to call after you've requested not to be
    called, or calls prior to 8:00 A.M. or after 9:00 P.M.?

If you answered yes to any of these questions, you may have been
the targeted victim of telemarketing fraud.

CHAPTER 16

On-Line and Ripped Off: Internet Fraud

The criminal is possibly the only human left who looks lovingly on society. He does not hanker to fight it, reform it or even rationalize it. He wants only to rob it.

BEN HECHT, SCREENWRITER, DIRECTOR, PLAYWRIGHT

Are you tired of trying to find good stock picks on your own? You can now subscribe to investor newsletters that offer stock recommendations over the Internet right on your own computer. Those newsletters will give you unbiased investment advice that has been researched and analyzed so you don't have to do the legwork. For instance, in 1998 *The Future Superstock (FSS)*, an Internet investment newsletter, claimed more than 100,000 subscribers. *FSS* recommended twenty-five micro-cap stocks and predicted they would double or triple in just months. A good, unbiased opinion based on solid research? Hardly.

What *FSS* failed to disclose was: (1) the receipt of more than $1.6 million in cash and stock from the companies profiled in the newsletter; (2) that little or no research was conducted on the recommended companies; (3) that *FSS* lied about the success of certain prior stock picks; and (4) that *FSS* sold several of the stocks it touted shortly after subscribers received the newsletter and the stocks' price increased. *FSS* was just one of forty-four companies that the SEC filed enforcement actions against in October 1998 for committing fraud over the Internet and deceiving investors.

The Internet offers thousands of products and services, making shopping and research easier than ever before. But although the Internet brings a wealth of information right into your own home at the push of a few buttons, it also has a dark side. If you're not careful, with the push of a few buttons, you can get ripped off. According to the Children's Partnership, a children's advocacy organization headquartered in Santa Monica, California, eleven million homes owned modem-equipped computers in late 1995. One year later that number had skyrocketed to eighteen million. It's becoming easier and cheaper to access the Internet. For a minimal investment, you can now purchase a cable box and cordless keyboard and get access to the Internet over your television set. As the number of Internet users grows, so will the number of con artists who go on-line to find their victims. The Internet will be the new frontier of investment fraud in amount of fraud and types of fraud perpetrated.

Con artists used to have to depend on the mail, advertisements, the phone, or personal meetings to rip you off. But using the phone or personal meetings meant conning one person at a time. Direct mail or advertisements can reach more people, but are expensive. With the popularity of the Internet came a fast, easy, and cheap way of reaching thousands of people at once. By posting a message on a bulletin board, carrying on a discussion in a chat room, or creating an Internet Web site, con men can reach tens of thousands of potential victims. And any type of fraud the con artists perpetrate on their victims over the phone or through the mail easily translates to the Internet.

Internet and on-line fraud is a burgeoning business. According to the National Consumer League's Fraud Information Center, reports of Internet and on-line fraud tripled from 1996 to 1997, and complaints have increased 600 percent since 1997. In fact, no one really knows how much on-line fraud is perpetrated, mainly because not everyone who is defrauded reports it—and those who do report it do so to myriad agencies, such as the SEC, Better Business Bureaus, attorney general offices, and others. Therefore, no single organization captures all the information needed to determine how much on-line fraud is perpetrated. The SEC alone reports that it receives about 120 complaints per day.

In December 1996, the FTC and law enforcement officials conducted what they called Internet Pyramid Surf Day, in which officials surfed the Internet looking for illegal pyramid schemes. In one day, they uncovered more than five hundred such schemes.

Types of Frauds

Pyramid schemes aren't the only types of fraud you'll find on-line. In fact, according to the National Consumer League's Fraud Information Center, in 1998 pyramid schemes were only the seventh most popular type of scheme offered by con artists. The top ten Internet scams, most of which have been discussed in other chapters, were:

1. *Auctions.* Actual auctions are held on-line where consumers can make bids for anything from appliances to computer equipment to antiques. The bidding may be open for a few days or weeks, and the highest bid wins. While the merchandise may be misrepresented or may never be delivered, another problem is that shills may drive up the bids to levels that are much higher than the actual value of the merchandise.

2. *Sale of general merchandise.* These offers arrive via e-mail or can be found in newsgroup postings, chat rooms, or Web sites. They offer all types of merchandise, from clothing to kitchenware to collectibles, but once paid for, the merchandise never arrives, is defective, or was misrepresented.

3. *Computer equipment/software.* Want to buy your computer equipment and software right over the Internet and save yourself a trip to the store? Be careful. What you buy and pay for may never be delivered, or may be completely misrepresented.

4. *Sales of Internet services.* The con artists promise to place ads on Web sites for a fee, sell passwords needed to access certain Web sites, or offer their victims free Internet access if they purchase software. Once the money is paid, the consumer never receives the services or products promised.

5. *Work-at-home schemes.* This type of fraud offers the opportunity to make money on a business you can start in your own home. Although the claim is that there are no up-front fees to

you, the business will probably require the purchase of specific equipment or software that you must buy from the con artist. These frauds often show up as unsolicited e-mails.

6. *Business opportunities/franchises.* Con artists offer all sorts of business opportunities but misrepresent the potential earnings that can be made. Or they may offer business assistance that's never provided.

7. *Pyramids and multilevel marketing schemes.* These are business deals in which victims pay to join programs with the promise of monetary returns from the membership fees paid by new recruits. Products may be offered as part of the membership, but no money is earned by selling products or services to consumers.

8. *Credit card offers.* Even if you have bad credit, there seems to be no lack of offers from people who are willing to issue you a credit card. Of course, you have to pay an advance fee. After the advance fee is paid, you never hear from them again.

9. *Advance fee loans.* If you need a loan, there are offers on-line, but if you're told that you have to pay an up-front fee prior to receiving the loan, it's a scam.

10. *Employment offers.* These con artists claim they can find you a job from listings of hidden employment offers that only they have access to. To qualify, you'll need to pay an up-front fee that is guaranteed to be refundable—don't believe it.

These are frauds that have been perpetrated by con artists for years, but there is one type of fraud the National Consumer League says it hadn't seen until the popularity of the Internet: private sales. The Internet has created a forum for people to trade or sell goods to each other on a one-on-one basis. The problem is that you don't know whom you are dealing with. If the person is a crook and never sends the goods to you after you've paid, it may not even be worth reporting to the authorities, because consumer protection laws at the state and federal levels don't apply to private sales. Most government consumer agencies don't even accept private sales complaints. Your only recourse in a private sale is to sue the person. But even if you locate the person, your chances are slim. If you're in New York and the other person is in Arizona, or even out of the country, trying to sue may be more difficult than it's worth. Of course, that's what the con artists count on.

Fraud From Abroad

On-line fraud can come from anywhere in the world, and you may not even realize it. Anyone can set up a dummy return address and appear to be operating out of one place when they're really somewhere else. One foreign scam lured consumers with the promise of lurid, erotic pictures that could be obtained by downloading a special image viewer. What consumers were not informed of was that if they used this special program, they would be disconnected from their local Internet carrier and connected to a foreign provider in Moldova in eastern Europe at a charge of two dollars per minute. The long-distance line would not be disconnected until the user's modem was switched off. Depending on the size of the user's appetite for erotic pictures, gigantic phone bills could be run up. The perpetrators of this crime collected a percentage of the foreign telephone carrier's revenues.

Looking for an investment? There are plenty of investment offers on the Internet that come from jurisdictions outside the United States. One company was trying to raise funds from private investors to finance the construction of an ethanol plant in the Dominican Republic. The investment promised a return of 50 percent or more, but there were no facts to back that up that promise. The literature boasted that the company had signed contracts with well-known companies. In reality, those contracts did not exist. Invest in this scheme, and you lose.

Often international trading investments offered on-line are extremely speculative. They may say they guarantee returns of up to 200 percent in less than a year, claim access to international traders who conduct riskless arbitrage, and claim that these are secret trading markets that only wealthy investors, large corporations, and overseas banks are privy to. In fact, they'll tell you that the market is so secret that if they find that you're trying to investigate it, you'll be expelled from the market permanently and not be allowed to invest—in reality, the best thing that could happen to you.

Or maybe your vice is gambling. No longer do you need

to travel to Las Vegas or Atlantic City. There are many Web sites that offer gambling, but many come from jurisdictions outside the United States. Some of the games are fixed so that it's impossible to win, while others allow you to win fairly large jackpots from time to time, but make it virtually impossible for you to collect your winnings. Either way, you lose.

Since many foreign countries have very different laws and legal systems from ours, if you become involved in a scam outside the jurisdiction of the United States, you will have much more difficulty recovering any losses or even figuring out where your money went.

Home-Grown Scams

You don't have to look overseas to find on-line scams. Domestic scams also proliferate. You can find offers to invest in eel farms, wireless cable projects, and all kinds of unregistered securities. Although some of these schemes may sound ludicrous, they generate millions of dollars for the con artists. For instance, two New Yorkers placed ads on the Internet claiming they could locate literary agents for aspiring writers who wanted to get their manuscripts published. While writers with hopes of getting published sent in money to get their manuscripts edited and published, these two people collected $5.5 million.

Then there are Internet offers for investments that don't exist. For example, two con artists working together collected more than $3.5 million by promising to double investors' money within four months. They were selling what they called prime bank securities—a security that doesn't even exist.

If you're scammed via the Internet, recourse is extremely difficult. Once you lose, you can assume you've lost for good. Just like with any other scheme, scam, or swindle, the chances of recovering lost money are practically nil. The time to worry about losing money is before you get involved. That doesn't mean you can't do business over the Internet. It just means you have to take precautions.

Deciphering Fraudulent Offers

Many fraudulent offers can be identified because they include a lot of hype:

> **"The subject of hundreds of magazine articles!"**
>
> **"As seen on TV!"**
>
> **"Learn how to make BIG $$$$$ MONEY in NO TIME AT ALL!!!!"**
>
> **"Earn profits while in the comfort of your own home!!"**

and the best one:

> **"This is not a scam!"**

Yeah, right. If you see lots of capital letters and exclamation points, unsubstantiated claims, and promises of big bucks, you may want to reconsider. Just because a Web site is flashy doesn't mean it's legitimate. Also, if the words "guaranteed" or "high return" or "safe as a CD" appear on the screen, be careful. No one can guarantee you'll make money on an investment, and the higher return you're offered, the more risk you're assuming. If the Web site offers you all the hype free of charge but you have to pay a fee to learn the details of the offer, forget it.

And don't believe the claim that these people have inside information about future mergers, acquisitions, or contracts that will drive up the price of a specific stock. If they really had inside information, they'd use it strictly for themselves and not advertise it on a Web site for thousands of people to see. More important, trading stock on inside information is illegal.

Some con artists don't even claim to have inside information. Take the case of Comparator Systems, an over-the-counter company that makes fingerprint identification systems. On May 3, 1996, an unidentified person, who presumably held the stock and wanted to sell it for a profit, bombarded Internet bulletin boards with messages that the stock would move from six cents per share to one dollar. More than a half-billion shares traded in less than a week, pushing the price to one dollar per share. NASDAQ officials halted trading in the stock; when it began trading again more than a month later, it opened at six cents per share. The con artists probably made a killing.

But if you don't believe one person, you may believe ten, right? Don't be so sure. Those ten people you see discussing how great a stock is may really be just one person trying to drum up interest in that stock to drive its price up. As soon as the price increases because you and several other victims purchased the stock, the con artist will dump his stock, driving the price back down and leaving you and your fellow investors with big losses.

A couple of years ago, the SEC investigated a market manipulation case in which the price of a stock moved dramatically because of messages posted on bulletin boards and in newsgroups. The authorities traced those messages back to a coffee shop with Internet access. Anyone could have used that terminal. Anonymity is a terrific advantage for the con artist. It gives him the ability to rip you off without your ever knowing who he is.

On-Line Fraud and Children

The Internet poses potential problems for young people. Children may inadvertently wander into a Web site that includes certain pictures, information, or language that is sexually explicit, violent, racially biased, or extremely commercial. Teenagers have been known to strike up relationships with strangers and even run away to meet their "new friend." Typically, however, when you think of being defrauded, you wouldn't expect your child to be the link.

Consider the case of a young girl who was participating in a chat room when someone on the line claiming to be the systems administrator said he needed her password immediately. She gave him the password, which ultimately gave him access to her father's credit card number. The con artist not only began making charges to the credit card, but also started sending obscene messages to the girl.

When the father learned about the problem, he cancelled his credit card and closed his Internet service provider account. The con artist realized what the father had done; he called the father and, posing as a representative from the Internet service provider, asked how to bill the remaining charges on the closed account. The father gave the swindler his new credit card number to close out the account, and the fraudulent charges began again.

Protecting Children From Internet Fraud

Parents need to know what their children are doing when on-line. If parents can't physically be with their children when on-line, there are a couple of ways they can restrict the material the child has access to:

- *Subscribe to on-line service parental controls.* Commercial on-line services such as America On-line, Prodigy, Microsoft Network, and CompuServe provide parental control mechanisms to block out inappropriate chat rooms and discussion groups. These features also give parents the ability to screen their child's e-mail.
- *Install parental controls software.* There is now software that parents can buy and install that blocks out certain categories of material or specific on-line sites, prevents children from giving out personal information, and restricts the time of day that a child can be on-line and how long he or she can be on-line.

Other products currently being developed will help parents restrict their children's on-line activities. But restricting your child's access doesn't have to restrict the fun and learning experience they can gain from the Internet. Some safe, interesting Web sites for kids include the following:

> Library of Congress: http://www.loc.gov
> White House Tour:
> http://www.whitehouse.gov/WH/kids/html/home.html
> NASA: http://spacelink.msfc.nasa.gov
> San Francisco's Exploratorium:
> http://www.exploratorium.edu/learning_studio/

For more information on children and the Internet, parents can contact the Children's Partnership and request its publications, including *The Parents' Guide to the Information Superhighway:*

The Children's Partnership
1351 Third Street Promenade, Suite 206
Santa Monica, California 90401-1321
1-310-260-1220
http://www.childrenspartnership.org

Protecting Yourself From Internet Fraud

If you decide to do business over the Internet, there are certain procedures you should follow:

- Be sure you know what company is making the offer, where it's located, and if it's legitimate.
- Ask your local consumer protection agency if the company needs to be licensed or registered and with what agency; then make sure it is. Any company that's raising less than one million dollars doesn't need to be registered with the SEC, but it is required to file a Form D, which includes the names and addresses of the company's owners. You can request a copy of the company's Form D from the SEC by calling 1-202-942-8090.
- If the company claims to be incorporated, call the office of the secretary of state and check it out. Ask whether the offering has been cleared for sale in your state. Call the Better Business Bureau and ask about the company's track record. However, if there are no complaints against the company, it doesn't mean that it's credible—it just means no one has bothered to complain. To learn more about new types of fraud, how to combat it, how to report it, and how to check a company's background, you can log on to the following organizations' Web sites:

    National Consumers League:
        www.natlconsumersleague.org
    National Fraud Information Center: www.fraud.org
    National Fraud Center: www.nationalfraud.com
    North American Securities Administrators Association:
        www.nasaa.org
    Better Business Bureau: www.bbb.org
    Better Business Bureau (to check a company's background): www.bbbonline.org

- Ask the company for additional information about any investment or product you're considering, and get as much information as you can in writing. If you can't verify the value and existence of an investment, don't invest. If you're purchasing a product over the Internet, do so from a reputable company you're familiar with. Before giving your credit card number, be sure you're on a secure site by looking for the unbroken key or the closed lock icon on your screen. Be sure the address starts with https rather than just http. Always download a copy of any offer you accept so that you have it in case of a future problem. Be sure to note the Web site address, the date, and time of the offer.
- As a precaution, change your password monthly, and keep it as complicated as possible by using a combination of numbers, letters, and symbols.

If you take all these precautions and never participate in any offer that appears to be fraudulent, you'll be free from on-line crime.

If you find you've become a victim of on-line fraud, report it immediately to your state securities authorities, your state's attorney general's office or consumer protection agency, the National Consumers League, the FTC, and the Better Business Bureau. The chances of recovering your losses will probably be slim, but by reporting the fraud, you may be able to save someone else from falling victim.

The jurisdictional problems for the authorities are horrendous when it comes to on-line fraud. The authority of each state securities board extends only to that state's borders. How can the authorities gather evidence and present it in court when the fraud is global? What does an investigator do when the company being investigated has its books and records hidden in a network in Stockholm and conducts all its financial transactions through an offshore bank in the Cayman Islands?

The Internet has changed the way people do business, gather information, and communicate with each other. The advantages of on-line access far outweigh the disadvantages, but some of those disadvantages can be deadly serious. While you don't have to give up your computer, you do have to be careful and use common sense. Just like with any type of transaction, be sure you:

- Know who you are dealing with.
- Don't give out personal information.
- Always check out any offer before you accept it.

By following these guidelines, you and your family can log on-line and use the enormous array of information available on the Internet to your advantage. I wish you happy and safe surfing!

Susan Grant, Director, National Fraud Information Center and Internet Fraud Watch Programs, National Consumer League, Washington, D.C.

People need to use the same critical analysis for promotions they see on the Internet or receive via e-mail that they apply to promotions made by telephone or door-to-door. Many of these scams are not new. They've been promoted in other ways for years, but are varied slightly to appeal to people on the Internet. They're just old wine in new bottles.

While the Internet makes it easier for people to communicate legitimately, it also makes it easier for crooks to reach people in a very low cost manner and to reach more people than ever before. Don't be lulled by the excitement of the Internet into thinking because it's a nice Web site, or because someone is willing to share an investment tip with you, that it's legitimate. People need to be cautious and think about on-line offers the same way they would before opening their door at home to a stranger.

It's difficult to know how much fraud is perpetrated over the Internet because not everyone complains and not everyone complains to the same place. The Better Business Bureau, federal agencies, state and local agencies, and other organizations all take complaints. No one place captures all that information. We try to help as many people as we can at the National Consumer League, but we're a not-for-profit organization and have the financial wherewithal to handle only so much. If read-ers are interested in making contributions to support our anti-telemarketing and Internet fraud programs, we're certainly interested. Their donations mean we can help more consumers and help stop some of the con artists before they target more victims. And that's our goal.

Checklist

Have you:

❏ Invested in an investment offer you located over the Internet without checking out the person or company making the offer, or the investment itself?

❏ Purchased goods or services or accepted other opportunities over the Internet without checking out the company or the person making the offer?

❏ Gambled on an Internet Web site?

❏ Given out credit card numbers or other personal information over an Internet Web site that was not secure?

❏ Continued to use the same password for your Internet access for months at a time?

❏ Neglected to monitor your children when they're using the Internet or not installed parental controls software?

If you answered yes to any of these questions, you could be the victim of Internet fraud.

PART EIGHT

HOW TO PROTECT YOURSELF

CHAPTER 17

How to Spot a Fraudulent Investment

An investment in knowledge pays the best interest.

BENJAMIN FRANKLIN, SOLDIER AND POLITICIAN

When Priscilla Deters of Productions Plus approached the National Friends (Quakers) Ministers Conference planning committee in the late 1980s, she offered what sounded like a great opportunity. She had a charitable trust in place that was worth $15.1 million, and she wanted to share the money with two or three charitable organizations that were working on projects that would help others. She wanted to help the Quakers, but first they had to prove to her that they were serious about their projects.

The first step was for them to give her five thousand dollars, which would go into a certificate of deposit in their name in a bank in California. That was earnest money, to prove they were really earnest about their projects. The deal was that the next year she would match that money, and they would then have ten thousand dollars in their account. The next year she would match that ten thousand dollars, making it twenty thousand dollars, and the following year she would match it again, making the twenty thousand dollars a total of forty thousand dollars.

The planning committee gave her approximately five

thousand dollars, and the following year she handed them a check for a whopping fifty thousand dollars—almost ten times their commitment and much more than they ever expected. She said it was for them to conduct their conference. That check made a believer out of the general superintendent of the Mid America Yearly Meeting (MAYM).

Deters then told the MAYM superintendent that she'd let them invest whatever amounts they wanted, and she would match it each year for three years. She included not only the district and local churches in her offer, but also individual church members. Before long, she had collected $439,200.

When the MAYM current trustees' terms expired, Leatha Hein became chair of the board of trustees. Hein hadn't personally invested with Productions Plus. She'd never even been approached about doing so. But now that she was a trustee, she had the opportunity to look at the situation more closely. That's when she knew something was terribly wrong. She found that Priscilla Deters had closed out the charitable trust that supposedly held $15.1 million. If the money existed, no one knew where it was. When the new trustees asked Deters how she was generating the amount of money it took to match what the church and its members were investing, she said she owned an electronic sign company and was using the profits from that.

Being a businesswoman, Hein knew the numbers didn't add up. The congregation had more than $400,000 invested. To match that each year for the next three years would require $2.8 million. Plus, Leatha knew that Deters was working with the Nazarenes, who were also investing money that was supposed to be matched. In the beginning, when Deters was matching five thousand dollars, it was plausible, but when you start talking about hundreds of thousands of dollars and she doubles that amount every year, the numbers become astronomical.

"There's no kind of business that can generate that kind of money unless it's drugs or money laundering," said Hein. "She'd have to have had an electronic sign on every corner in the whole country."

While the church and its members did manage to make several withdrawals from their accounts between 1989 and 1992, the withdrawals soon dried up. Then the financial reports they had been receiving stopped coming. When they couldn't withdraw their money, the trustees told Deters they were considering calling the authorities. Her response was that she had ample money and would begin making payments soon, but for the time being she was trying to separate the wheat from the chaff. If the Quakers and their church turned out to be wheat, they'd get their money. But she said she'd give no money at all to anyone who went to the securities commission or cooperated with the authorities. Hein convinced the trustees to involve the authorities, who investigated and found the whole program to be a Ponzi scheme wrapped in affinity fraud.

In the end, the Quakers lost $85,000. Their losses weren't as bad as those suffered by others because they were one of the first ones involved in this Ponzi scheme. Part of the money that Productions Plus had collected from the Nazarenes and others had been used to make payments to the Quakers to make the whole scheme look realistic. Productions Plus was operating the same scam in twenty-one states.

Deters went on trial in Kansas in February 1998 for the charges against her only in that state. On May 21, 1998, she was fined and sentenced to eleven years and three months in prison. Indictments in other states were still pending.

Leatha Hein knew that an offer that looks too good to be true probably is, so she never invested any of her own money with Deters. Unfortunately, others did, and they lost.

No One Is Safe

Clearly not all con men are men. We can't be lulled into complacency just because someone wears a dress and high heels. But it can be hard to be suspicious of someone, regardless of gender, who sounds so convincing and even follows through with promises for a time. But all con artists are convincing. Whether it's affinity fraud, Ponzi schemes, pyramid schemes, telemarketing scams, or Internet fraud, it'll sound convincing.

No one, regardless of age, level of wealth, or amount of investment experience, can ever be 100 percent sure he or she won't end up the victim of investment fraud. Maybe you think you're too savvy an investor to get caught up in investment fraud.

If someone told you she'd double your money every year, you'd know in a heartbeat that something was wrong. The reality is that while you may be a savvy investor with a lot of experience, you'd be dealing with a savvy con artist with a lot of experience. These people may be dishonest and untrustworthy, but they're professional at what they do. They know how to convince even the staunchest skeptic.

How to Check Out an Investment

We all want to maximize the returns we make on our investments, and we all want to take advantage of any legitimate money-making propositions that may come our way. With care, you can accomplish both. Trying to avoid fraud doesn't mean you should never make an investment, never deal with a new investment professional, or never dabble in new types of investments. It does mean asking questions, checking out the people and companies you do business with, and taking time to study, research, and understand any investment you consider.

Checking out an investment offer can be time-consuming and may even involve some minor expenses. But consider the consequences of not spending that time, effort, and money. The money you may lose to a fraudulent investment will take you a lot more time and effort to earn back. That should be enough impetus.

If you know how to identify a suspicious investment or salesperson's pitch, you'll save yourself a lot of time. There are red flags you can watch for and steps you can take to help reduce your chances of becoming a victim. Look for the following red flags when considering an investment.

- *A high rate of return.* If most investments in the current marketplace offer a rate of return in the range of 7 to 10 percent and someone offers an investment that pays 18 percent, that's a red flag. Remember, the higher the return, the higher the risk.
- *Guaranteed, no-risk investment.* A "no-risk investment" is a contradiction in terms. All investments have some level of risk. While some con artists will claim their investment carries

no risk, others may try to make their pitches sound a little more viable by admitting that the investment does carry a small level of risk. But they'll quickly follow up that statement by telling you that the risk is minimal and the huge return you'll realize far outweighs any risk. Don't believe it.

- *Urgency to invest.* The typical story goes that this is such a terrific investment that it's selling out quickly. If you want to get in on it, you'd better make a decision right now. To get you to make a quick decision, the salesperson may even belittle you with statements such as "If you can't make a decision, I have other investors who can. I can't waste my time with someone who doesn't have the foresight to take advantage of an opportunity like this." In some cases, the con artist may offer to send a courier to your house or office to pick up your check—supposedly for your convenience. The real reason for this urgency is that the con artist needs to get your money quickly so he can get out of town and stay one step ahead of the authorities. And sending a courier to pick up your check not only gets the money to him faster, but it also saves him from facing mail fraud charges if he's caught.

Those are three red flags that should make you suspicious when dealing with an investment salesperson. If those red flags aren't apparent or aren't enough to make you hang up the phone and walk away, then it's time to start asking some questions.

At this point in the conversation, you can be sure that so far, all the questions have been asked by the salesperson. And you can bet you've answered yes to every one of them because they're all framed in language that makes you look like an idiot if you answer no. For example:

- Would you like to make a lot of money in a short time with no risk? (Yes!)
- Would you be interested in finding a great investment opportunity? (Yes!)
- Does 35 percent annual return sound good to you? (Yes!)

Everyone's in agreement so far! Now it's *your* turn to be the questioner.

Following are questions you should pose to any investment salesperson. As you ask the questions, take notes and keep track of everything you're promised so you have a record in case you later end up in a dispute:

- *"Where did you get my name?"* The answer may be that it came from a "select list of experienced and intelligent investors." That means he probably got your name from the phone book. If you've been defrauded before, your name may be on someone's list of prey that gets passed around from one scamster to the next. Most reputable salespeople will tell you how they were referred to you.

- *"How risky is this investment?"* If he claims there's no risk or that the risk is extremely minimal, that raises Red Flag No. 2. If you foresee specific risks that would be inherent in this type of investment, ask about those, and be sure the answers aren't vague and lack common sense. If the con artist has given you written risk disclosures but plays them down as being routine formalities, don't believe it. When your money is gone, he'll use those risk disclosures against you, claiming you knew what risks existed.

An honest salesperson doesn't want to hide the risks, because he wants to be sure the risk level of the investment fits the investor. That's because of Rule 405, set forth by the New York Stock Exchange, stating that all brokers must "know their clients," because an investment that is suitable for one client may not be appropriate for another. Due to Rule 405, stockbrokers who sell clients investments that are far too risky to suit their situations will be reprimanded. Therefore, the stockbroker wants you to know the risks and assess whether they fit your investment needs.

- *"How much are the fees and commissions on this investment?"* You want specific answers to this question. For instance, are there interest charges, storage charges, profit-sharing arrangements with management, front-end fees, back-end fees, promoter's profits, marketing expense fees, early withdrawal fees? Are commissions 2 percent, 4 percent, or 6 percent? What percentage of your money will be invested? If you invest two thousand dollars, will five hundred dollars of it be paid to the salesperson for commissions and fees, leaving you with only a fifteen-hundred-dollar investment to generate a return? Do early withdrawal fees start at 5 percent and decrease each year? Make a list of all the costs associated with the investment.

- *"Is the investment traded on a U.S. exchange?"* Not all types of investments trade on an exchange, but almost no fraudulent ones trade over a U.S. exchange. Exchanges have rules in place to help ensure that investments are legitimate, and when they aren't, sanctions are imposed. If the investment isn't traded over an exchange, it may not be very liquid. Ask if there are other buyers to whom you can resell your investment when you're ready, how you resell your investment, and what costs will be associated with resale.

- *"Could you send me documentation?"* Every investment, whether it's a stock, a bond, or a private limited partnership, should be backed up with some sort of documentation, such as an annual report or a prospectus, that explains what the investment is and how it works. A reputable salesperson will give you this information, and in some cases is bound by law to be sure you have that material in hand prior to making the investment. If a salesperson is unwilling to provide documentation, that's an indication of a scam.

The con artist doesn't want to send you documentation for three primary reasons:

1. He doesn't want anything in writing that his victims could use later.

2. He doesn't want to send anything through the mail because he could then face mail fraud charges.

3. He doesn't want to take the time to send you materials to read. (Remember Red Flag No. 3: urgency.)

In some cases, the bold con artist may be willing to send you a small brochure he has created that lists the merits of the investment. But anyone can have a few slick brochures printed. That doesn't mean the information contained in them is necessarily true. And if he wants your checking account number, credit card number, or Social Security number to make proper identification or to verify that you're a reputable investor prior to sending you the information, forget it. No investment professional needs that information to discuss an investment with you or to send you documents. Although your Social Security number will be required if you open an account, it should be supplied only on a written application. If you supply any of those numbers at the discussion stage, you'll find your checking account drained, your credit card balance sky high, and possibly your identity lost (see Chapter 12).

- *"Could you explain this investment to my attorney, accountant, or adviser?"* Look back at Red Flag No. 3. The salesperson agrees that you have a great idea, but there's no time to consult with anyone else because a decision has to be made right now. The last thing the con artist wants is to have a professional adviser hear about this investment and not only advise you against it but maybe turn him in to the authorities.

A reputable salesperson would certainly be willing to explain an investment to your adviser. In fact, he would probably prefer to explain it to someone who will totally understand the investment and advise you accordingly because that takes some of the pressure off him if there is a dispute later.

- *"What types of statements do you provide?"* When you open an account at a brokerage firm, it will send you a monthly statement that lists each asset in your portfolio and any buy and sell transactions that took place during that month. When you buy a company's stock, that company will send you an annual report with audited financial statements and three quarterly reports each year.

If you purchase this investment, will you receive statements that reflect your holdings, transactions, and the addition of interest or dividends? Will those statements be monthly, quarterly, or annual? Will you receive reports as to the progress of the investment? Will they include audited financial statements?

- *"How will your rate of return be calculated?"* Ask the salesperson how to calculate your rate of return, and be sure you can comprehend the explanation. If it's so complicated that a year from now you can't remember how to calculate it, it'll be tough to dispute any claim that you didn't receive the proper amount of interest or dividends.

- *"How long has your company been in business, and what is its track record?"* Just because a business is new doesn't mean it's fraudulent. Just because a business has been around for several years doesn't mean it's reputable. If the company has been around a while, ask for written information about its track record, and check it out. If the company is new, the person you're talking to certainly isn't. He has to have a past that you can check out, and you should do that. Just because someone sounds professional, confident, and knowledgeable doesn't mean he's honest. To avoid becoming a victim of fraud, you have to remain skeptical.

Also, ask for the names of the firm's principals and officers, and check them out at the same time. If you're told the principals and officers wish to remain anonymous, that's a problem.

You can check out an investment firm and an investment adviser by calling the Better Business Bureau or your state securities agency. You can get the appropriate number for your state by calling the North American Securities Administrators Association at 1-202-737-0900. If there have been no complaints filed, however, don't assume the person is legitimate. It may just mean that people who were defrauded were too embarrassed to report it; the victims haven't yet realized they were scammed; or this joker just got to town and your number was the first one he dialed.

You should also call the National Association of Securities Dealers Public Disclosure Phone Center at 1-800-289-9999. Give the name of the investment adviser and the firm, and they can give you information as to the firm's and the individual's disciplinary record. That information can also be found on-line at www.nasdr.com.

Ask the salesperson what governmental or industry regulatory agencies have jurisdiction over the company; then call those agencies and check out the company. Find out if the securities are registered and if a prospectus and annual report have been filed with the securities regulators. If you're told the investment is structured to exempt the securities of the company from registration, the company is probably trying to avoid contact with the regulators.

If the investment involves futures contracts, the Commodity Futures Trading Commission or the National Futures Association should have jurisdiction. If you're dealing with securities, the regulatory arm is the SEC or the National Association of Securities Dealers (NASD).

- *"Can you give me references?"* Obviously, the name of any individuals the salesperson gives you will be suspect. If he's a con artist, he'll probably give you the name and number of one of his cohorts. Instead, ask for names of well-known banks, brokerage firms, law firms, or accounting firms the person has worked with that will provide a reference.

If you're dealing with a con artist, you probably won't get answers to all these questions. In fact, you probably won't get answers to any of them. What you'll get are vague responses and then a quick change of topic back to what a great return you'll get on your money with this investment. From the information you do gather or from the information the salesperson refuses to share with you, you should be able to make a determination as to the viability of the investment.

After You Invest

If, after asking all the questions, you decide to invest, monitor your investment regularly. Be sure you receive the documents or financial statements you were promised and any regularly scheduled payments of interest or dividends. Call the salesperson from time to time to check in and find out what's happening with the investment. If your accessibility to the person suddenly fades because he's always on another line, out of town, or with a customer and he doesn't return calls, you may have a problem. Accept that you may have been duped, read Chapter 18, and start doing a little reporting to the agencies.

Leatha Hein, Trustee of Mid America Yearly Meeting of Friends (Quaker Church), Valley Center, Kansas

Priscilla Deters of Productions Plus had so many people in our church duped that when the board of trustees began investigating her and accused her of fraud, a lot of the people in our church got angry. That's how much they believed in her. When she wouldn't let us make any withdrawals from our account, she always had an excuse as to why she didn't have the money available at that time. The other church members trusted her so much that they said we should leave her alone and let her work her plan. They believed she'd come through with the money.

At the trial, where I testified against Deters, some of our pastors even testified on her behalf. But the prosecuting attorneys had physical evidence where they showed that on a specific date she received a check and immediately wrote a check to someone else. On another date, she received a check, and she bought a new car. And on still another date, she received a check and made a down payment on a house for her son.

Even with that hard evidence, some of our people still believed in her and thought the authorities were making it all up. People can really get duped. I think some of them would give her more money today if they could.

Most of our church's investments in the past had been with investment firms that met the regulations of the law and the SEC. We should have had investment guidelines in place saying we'll invest a portion of our portfolio in stocks, bonds, or real estate, and stuck to that plan. If we had done that, we would not have gotten into this mess.

Checklist

Have you been:

❑   Offered an investment that pays an extremely high rate of return, is guaranteed and carries no risk, and is available only if you accept the offer immediately?

❑   Offered an investment, but the salesperson won't answer

your questions satisfactorily and refuses to send you written documentation explaining the investment?

❏ Encouraged to purchase an investment without first being asked a series of questions as to your net worth, income, and investment experience?

❏ Asked for your Social Security number by an investment salesperson before you've agreed to open an account or purchase an investment?

❏ Refused access to a salesperson from whom you purchased an investment?

If you answered yes to any of these questions, you're probably dealing with a con artist who's selling fraudulent investments.

CHAPTER 18

Fighting Back: Where to Turn When You've Been Defrauded

I want to make this place so unpleasant that they won't even think about doing something that could bring them back.

JOE ARPAIO, SHERIFF OF MARICOPA COUNTY, CALIFORNIA

As a commercial fisherman, Mike made a good living. Of course, he had to be away from his Washington state home six months out of the year, and that was difficult. But he and his wife managed despite the fact that when he was out to sea, they had only limited communication using the shortwave radio.

During one of his stints at home, Mike got a call from a stockbroker in New York. The broker told him that if he wanted a good return on his money, there were five stocks he should buy. He said all five companies had good performance track records, and the stocks were guaranteed to make him a lot of money. In fact, the stockbroker said he had even bought some of these stocks himself and had sold some to his own brother.

Before he went back to sea, Mike invested a little money in each of the five recommended stocks. After he left and went back on the ship, Mike's wife received a call from the stockbroker. He said he had just talked to Mike over the shortwave radio and that he had asked him to call her and tell her to send the stockbroker a check for twenty thousand dollars to buy more stock. Mike's wife was familiar with the stockbroker, and she was a very trusting person. She believed him and sent the money. She also honored subsequent requests for money that "Mike asked her to send" via the stockbroker's request. In all, the stockbroker ended up with seventy thousand dollars of Mike's money.

When Mike came back from sea and found out what had happened, he complained to the broker and the brokerage firm's compliance department. When they weren't willing to right the wrong, he found representation and filed an arbitration case against the broker. Through this process, he recovered his seventy thousand dollars, plus interest. The arbitrators even made a referral to law enforcement officials, who eventually pulled the stockbroker's license.

If you become the target of fraud, immediately try to resolve the problem through the offending stockbroker and the brokerage firm's compliance department. During the process, keep notes and follow up every conversation with a letter outlining what was discussed. If you get no resolution, report it to the SEC. The SEC will analyze the complaint, contact the broker and the brokerage firm, and try to resolve the problem. This process could take as much as three to four months. If the SEC finds no resolution, you have two legal processes you can pursue: mediation and arbitration.

Mediation

Mediation is an informal process in which a single mediator assists the two parties in determining a mutually agreeable resolution to a dispute. The mediator doesn't make a final decision and cannot impose a settlement on the parties. Instead, he helps the two parties create a solution on their own by helping them move the focus from their emotions to the real issues of the situation. During the process, the two parties meet with the mediator, jointly and separately, tell their stories, try to understand the other party's position, and, with the assistance of the mediator, come to a decision. If either party becomes dissatisfied with the mediator, he or she can stop the mediation process at any time.

Mediation is fast, cost-effective, private, and confidential.

There is no winner or loser because the parties come to a mutually agreeable solution. The process can be completed in as little as three months. Mediation is a voluntary process; therefore, both parties must agree to it before the process can take place.

The process of mediation is fairly new; it became an option for wronged investors only in the mid-1990s. In 1997, there were 865 mediation cases heard. Approximately 79 percent, or 683, of those cases were resolved. Cases that aren't resolved through mediation typically go to arbitration.

Arbitration

Arbitration is a method of dispute resolution in which impartial persons, known as arbitrators, hear a case and make a final, binding, and nonappealable decision. To be eligible for arbitration, an investor must file an arbitration claim within six years from the date of the event that caused the dispute. Suitability and churning are the issues that are brought to securities arbitration most frequently.

When it comes to securities disputes, due to the 1987 U.S. Supreme Court ruling of *Shearson v. McMahon*, investors cannot sue brokers, and, in fact, they even sign away their rights to do so when they open a brokerage account. In actuality, due to the speed and low cost of arbitration, that ruling was good for investors. Going through the courts and having to face appeals is a time-consuming, extremely expensive proposition. Arbitration saves the investor that time and expense.

If you enter the arbitration process, you can represent yourself, or you can hire representation. But the old saying "A person who represents himself has a fool for a client" is probably accurate. According to Paul N. Young, founder and CEO of Securities Arbitration Group and National Mediators Group in Marina Del Rey, California, investors with representation win far more money a greater percentage of the time than investors who choose to represent themselves.

For instance, Young had a client who was sixty-eight years old when he retired from his job as a truck driver for a dairy after twenty-eight years of service. Harvey, who had a tenth-grade education, had never been compensated more than ten dollars an hour during his career, but early in his life, he had managed to save his money and buy a small home in the suburbs of Los Angeles. By the time he retired, that home had appreciated substantially in value. Having a heart condition and a seriously ill wife, he decided to sell the home and purchase a small condo. That transaction netted him a $100,000 profit, which he planned to invest and live off for the rest of his life.

A short time after Harvey received the $100,000, he got a call from a stockbroker licensed with a large Wall Street brokerage firm who convinced him to buy a long-term, high-risk, nonliquid limited partnership for—you guessed it—$100,000. His nest egg was gone.

Harvey asked Young to represent him, and they filed an arbitration case. They won an award of $180,000: $100,000 return of his investment, $30,000 interest on his money, and $50,000 punitive damages. While Harvey doesn't know how he would have fared if he had tried to fight the case by himself, there's a possibility that he may not have won. But there's an extremely large possibility that he never would have won the $50,000 in punitive damages on his own, because the award of punitive damages is fairly rare. Young believes that Harvey may not have recovered any money if he had not had firm, focused representation, because brokerage firms vigorously defend these cases.

As Harvey's case shows, having representation is probably wise. A novice who has no knowledge of how the process works and who the players are is no match for the brokerage firm's attorneys. For instance, after an investor files an arbitration claim, the arbitrators are appointed, a process in which the investor has input. During the process of choosing the arbitrators, the investor can have one arbitrator on the panel replaced. A reason for making that request may be that the investor believes the arbitrator has a bias toward the brokerage firm. But the novice doesn't know the individual arbitrators as the brokerage firm representatives do and therefore doesn't know which arbitrator would serve him best. A representative who works with the arbitrators frequently would know.

After the panel of arbitrators is chosen, the parties prepare for the hearing by pulling together pertinent documents and contacting witnesses to testify. The key to winning an arbitration case is in the preparation, because the burden of proof is on the investor.

It's extremely important to be sure you're presenting all the evidence pertaining to the case. If you're ruled against in the arbitration process and later discover more evidence that would help your case, you're out of luck. The arbitrators are not allowed to reconsider a decision even if new evidence has been found. In gathering evidence, if you haven't kept copies of relevant documents, such as your monthly account statements, the brokerage firm is required to supply them.

At the hearing, which can last from half a day to six days depending on the number of witnesses to be heard, the parties present their cases to the arbitrators through testimony and documentary evidence. Within thirty business days after the hearing, the parties are notified of the arbitrators' decision by mail. Reasons behind the final decision are not revealed. If the award is in your favor, it will specify the amount of the award and the terms of payment.

The complete arbitration process takes approximately one year. The cost of arbitration is on a sliding scale, but for claims under one thousand dollars there is a fifteen-dollar filing fee and a fifteen-dollar hearing session deposit. At the other end of the spectrum, for a claim of five million dollars, those fees jump to three hundred dollars and fifteen hundred dollars, respectively, plus the cost of representation.

Ninety percent of all securities arbitrations are filed with the National Association of Securities Dealers (NASD), and the other 10 percent are filed with the arbitration departments of the various exchanges. In 1980, there were only 318 arbitration cases filed with the NASD. In 1997, according to Young, there were 5,997 arbitration cases filed with the NASD, and 60 percent of those cases were found in favor of investors.

Investors who seek representation can contact the American Bar Association (ABA) or the Public Investors Arbitration Bar Association (PIABA) for a referral. Contact information for the NASD Dispute Resolution Offices, the ABA, and PIABA offices is given in the Appendix.

If you are wronged by a stockbroker, the processes of mediation and arbitration are fair and efficient opportunities for you to tell your story and get the problem resolved. Typically an investor starts both the mediation and the arbitration processes at the same time. If the case is solved through mediation, the arbitration case can be easily terminated.

Mediation and arbitration were created so that investors could have a forum where they can present their case and obtain a fair and equitable resolution. If you have been defrauded, take advantage of that opportunity—you owe it to yourself.

Paul N. Young, Founder and CEO, Securities Arbitration Group, National Mediators Group, Marina Del Rey, California

Every hour in this country a new securities arbitration case is filed. Each one of those cases represents a family, a person, a situation, someone who has been or thinks he or she has been victimized. Those people can fight back by finding good representation and using the processes of mediation and arbitration.

Most people who have been defrauded have twin emotions— anger and embarrassment—and it can be difficult to get past those emotions. Some people simply can't fight back due to their age or the emotional distress involved. If someone is eighty-five years old and in a nursing home, for example, it may be emotionally and physically draining for that person to go through the process.

But if you have a claim with merit and can stand the rigors, you're a fool not to fight back. If you've been victimized once, your failure to fight back means you lose twice—guaranteed. You have to fight back, and you have to do it immediately.

Of the cases that come to me, I accept only one out of fifty. Half of the cases I turn away have no merit. If your stockbroker told you the truth and the investments he recommended were suitable for you, you don't have a case. The other cases I reject are sad to see because they're claims that have merit, but the person didn't act within the six-year eligibility window from the time the fraudulent investment was first sold to them. If they had taken action right away, they would have at least had the opportunity to reclaim their losses.

My firm offers the only nongovernmental securities fraud hot line in the country. Our number is 1-800-222-4724, and people are free to call for advice on their cases. Every day we get calls from people who believe they've been defrauded. We try to help as many as we can.

In the past twenty years, I've seen cases where brokerage firms will spend fifty thousand dollars to avoid paying a wronged investor twenty-five thousand dollars. It doesn't make sense, but they typically don't pay claims without a fight. But through mediation and arbitration, investors have the ability to fight back. I recommend they do it.

Checklist

When trying to resolve a dispute with your stockbroker, have you:

❑   Attempted to resolve the problem directly with the stockbroker or with the brokerage firm's compliance department?

❑   Kept notes of all conversations with your stockbroker or other personnel regarding the complaint?

❑   Followed up phone calls regarding the complaint with a letter outlining what was discussed?

❑   Attempted to resolve the problem through mediation?

❑   Filed an arbitration claim within six years from the date of the event that caused the dispute?

If you answered yes to these questions, you're probably well prepared to fight back.

PART NINE

WHOM CAN YOU TRUST?

CHAPTER 19

Finding and Working With a Trustworthy Stockbroker

Some men climb the ladder of success one rung at a time to find it's leaned against the penitentiary wall.

ANONYMOUS

If you needed to hire a stockbroker and you learned that down the street from where you work there's an office of a major, big-name brokerage firm that has offices in every major city across the country, would you use that firm? Before you opened an account with this well-known firm, would you check it out? The answers to those two questions are "probably so" and "probably not," respectively. Certainly, you may think, a major brokerage firm and a stockbroker who works for that firm don't need to be checked out.

On the contrary, don't be lulled into complacency just because a brokerage firm is practically a household name. Proof that you could be making a major mistake is the story of Fannie Victor. Kurt Eichenwald relates Victor's story in his book *Serpent on the Rock* (1995).

Victor was an eighty-year-old retiree from New York who moved to Scottsdale, Arizona, in 1985. With the help of her daughter and son-in-law, she bought a condominium and arranged for a mortgage. She then invested her life savings, about

$100,000, with a stockbroker at Prudential-Bache Securities, a well-known brokerage firm. The stockbroker stressed that the proper investments for Victor's situation were ones that were safe and secure and generated income. He invested the money for her and told her she would receive $792.67 a month from her investments.

But instead of coming monthly as she was promised, the checks came quarterly, and they were for far less than what was promised. Finally, the checks stopped coming at all. In November 1990, Victor's daughter confronted the stockbroker and found that her mother's funds had been invested in limited partnerships that were risky, were performing poorly, and for which there was no real market where she could sell them. Because she wasn't receiving the income she had been promised, Victor was far behind on her mortgage payments. She finally had to face the fact that foreclosure on her condominium was her only option.

Victor was not the only investor who became a victim of Prudential-Bache Securities' unscrupulous business activities in the 1980s. Hundreds of thousands of other people lost millions of dollars. In fact, Prudential-Bache Securities had packaged and sold more than $8 billion worth of risky limited partnerships that collapsed.

Despite the Prudential-Bache Securities scandal of the 1980s, the truth is that the majority of all stockbrokers in business today are honest and trustworthy people. Unfortunately, some are not. The problem is that you can't tell which are which. By doing a little homework before you hire a stockbroker, however, you can cut your chances of ending up with one who's going to rip you off.

Before you start looking for that broker, you need to do a little work so that when you talk to a broker, you know what you want. First think through your financial needs and determine your investment objectives. Are you investing for your retirement, to send your child to college, or to buy a house? Will you need the money in six months, two years, or twenty years? Do you want to build a portfolio of investments that are fairly conservative? Are you looking primarily to preserve your capital and earn income from dividends and interest? Or do you want to build a more aggressive portfolio that will give you good growth potential?

You don't necessarily have to have an asset allocation plan all worked out before you find a stockbroker, but you do need to know your basic investment objectives, and you should commit them to paper.

Choosing a Stockbroker

You're now ready to start seeking out a stockbroker. You'll quickly find, however, that most stockbrokers are not called stockbrokers anymore. Titles range from *registered representative* to *account executive* to *broker* to *financial adviser*. Don't let it throw you—they're all stockbrokers.

Don't be impressed by titles such as senior vice president or chief investment vice president. Those titles may mean nothing. In fraudulent brokerage firms, those titles are handed out to trainees who've been on the job two days because they evoke a belief that the person is a seasoned stockbroker who meets certain standards. That may be true at some brokerage firms but not at others. Ignore titles. They can be deceptive.

Categories of Brokerage Houses

Prior to 1975, stockbrokers were all full-service stockbrokers who charged the same amount of commissions. But on May 1, 1975, the SEC mandated an end to all fixed commissions. That opened the door for discount brokerage houses. For a while, there was a clear delineation between full-service brokerage firms and discount brokerage firms. Over the years, though, the whole industry has become a shade of gray. Although no two brokerage firms tend to be alike anymore, there are three basic categories: full service, discount, and deep discount.

A *full-service brokerage firm* is exactly what its name implies: It gives you full service. Do you want to work with one specific broker? Do you want that broker to send you research reports, call you with investment ideas, suggest when you might consider selling a stock, help ensure that your portfolio is well diversified? If so, you need a full-service broker. All of these services will save you time and effort, but where there's service, there's cost. Every time you buy or sell an investment, you'll be charged a commission. The amount depends on the investment you're purchasing, the size of the investment, and the size of your overall account.

When *discount brokerage firms* first appeared, about all they did was buy and sell stocks and bonds for their customers. Over the years, that has changed. There are now discount firms that may be willing to send you third-party research reports such as Value Line reports and Standard & Poor's reports. At some discount firms you may even work with one specific stockbroker. The level of service offered at the discount firms varies greatly, and so do commission amounts. Investors can almost customize the level of service they want and the amount of commissions they're willing to pay by shopping around and finding out what services the various firms offer.

No service, but cheap: That's what you get with *deep discount brokerage firms*. But the words *no service* may really mean no service. In fact, when you want to buy or sell stock, you may not even talk to a person. You may have to input your trades using a touch-tone telephone or a computer. Don't try to ask anyone for a Value Line report or for a stock recommendation. That's not their job. They transact your buy and sell orders only, but they do it cheaply.

The level of commissions varies greatly among these three types of brokerage firms. If you buy one hundred shares of a thirty-dollar stock, you could pay three hundred dollars or twelve dollars or anywhere in between as a commission. Which type of brokerage firm you choose depends on how much assistance you want from your broker. If you don't have time to get your own research reports, if you like to have someone give you stock suggestions, and if you like to have an extra pair of eyes monitoring your portfolio, the extra cost of a full-service brokerage firm may be money well spent. But if you typically come up with your own investment ideas, have time to go to the library to get research reports, and feel comfortable that you're doing a good job monitoring your portfolio, why spend the extra money? There is, however, another option: Use both. You could open an account with a deep discount brokerage firm and use that account to buy securities you've discovered, researched, and made a decision to buy on your own. If no one gave you the recommendation and no one spent time helping you research it, or supplied you with information, buy it from a deep discount firm.

You can also open an account with a full-service brokerage firm and use it to buy securities that have been recommended by your broker or securities that he helped you research. There's no harm in using two different types of brokerage firms. There is, however, harm in using the full-service broker's recommendation, research, time, and effort and then buying the stock from another firm. That's basically stealing from the broker. There are enough con men, swindlers, and scamsters in this book; we don't want to add you to the list. If you expect your stockbroker to play fair with you, it's only right that you play fair with him.

Meeting the Stockbroker

After you've decided which type of brokerage firm you want to use, find a couple that fit that category. The best way is to get a personal recommendation from your accountant, attorney, or other adviser. If that isn't possible, look in the Yellow Pages or listen to ads on television or radio, or read business magazines and newspapers.

Call two or three firms. Explain that you're in need of a stockbroker and ask for whatever information is available on the firm, such as brochures, clippings, and commission schedules. After you get the information and read through it, choose one or two firms you think you'd like working with. Then get dressed and comb your hair—you've got a business meeting you have to get to. It's time to meet these people face-to-face. And don't say you don't have time—it's important.

If you needed brain surgery, you wouldn't call a doctor you never met and schedule an appointment for surgery. You wouldn't know if this guy was working out of a major hospital downtown and had access to all the latest medical equipment, or if he was working out of a back room in his house with a thermometer and switchblade. You'd also want to know what this guy's like. Maybe he's a coldhearted person who has no compassion for his patients. You'd definitely want to go to his office, see where he works, find out about his credentials, and meet him. You'd also expect him to want a little information about you before he started cutting.

The same is true with investing your money. You want to meet this person you'll be turning your life savings over to. You want to see where he works, see how he works, and find out if you feel comfortable with him.

Call the firms you've identified and say you'd like to come in and discuss possibly using its services. (If it's a deep discount firm you've chosen, this option isn't available.) The firm will assign a specific stockbroker to meet with you. Don't expect an invitation to lunch, but you should get an invitation to come in for a free-of-charge half-hour meeting. Some firms and stockbrokers may not meet with you. Time is money, and if they think your account is too small to warrant spending time with you, they may refuse. Whether you want to work with that firm or person is your choice.

The goal of this meeting is to get to know the stockbroker, ask a few questions, and answer a few questions. The stockbroker shouldn't try to sell you anything at this point. Instead, he should ask about your investment goals and objectives. Are you investing for your retirement in forty years or to send your child to college in ten years or to buy a house in a couple of years?

You should ask about the stockbroker's investing philosophy. If you have a buy-and-hold philosophy and the stockbroker is a speculator who wants to buy stocks and sell them as soon as they go up a little in price, the relationship won't work. Ask who the broker's other clients are. If he's used to working with millionaires and you have twenty thousand dollars to invest, this may not be the right broker for you. Ask for a commission schedule, and find out if there are other fees, such as annual management or maintenance fees. Some firms charge inactivity fees if there aren't a certain number of transactions processed in an account during the year.

Ask about the person's professional experience, education, and background. Was he a marketing executive for a computer company until six months ago? If so, will he be seasoned enough in investing to give you the service you need? Ask about the firm's hours, access to research reports, and other services, such as a phone service or an on-line service you can use to access your account or make trades. Ask if the firm is a member of the Securities Investor Protection Corporation (SIPC), the organization that provides some client protection when a brokerage firm becomes insolvent. Of course, you can't depend on the SIPC to reimburse you if a stockbroker steals your money.

After you've spent time with the stockbroker and asked all your questions, you should know whether you feel comfortable with that person. If you feel he was willing to take time to answer your questions, was able to explain everything so it was under-standable, and was genuinely interested in listening to your needs, then this person is a possibility. But you're not done with your homework yet.

Investigating the Broker and the Firm

Call the National Association of Securities Dealers (NASD) Public Disclosure Phone Center at 1-800-289-9999. Give the name of the stockbroker and the brokerage firm, and the NASD can tell you if either one has had any disciplinary actions taken against them. If there are no problems, the association will tell you that over the phone. If there are, it will send you a listing of the disciplinary actions taken. If the person or the firm has been fined and cen-sured in the past, you may want to look elsewhere. Of course, if there are no actions taken, that doesn't mean the person has been on the straight and narrow. It could just mean that no one has reported any problems. You can also call your local Better Business Bureau and inquire about any investor complaints about the bro-ker or the firm.

And finally, call the state securities agency and ask if the brokerage firm and the stockbroker are both licensed or registered to sell securities in your state and whether any complaints have been filed against them. Ask for a copy of the Central Registration Depository (CRD) printout for the broker, which includes informa-tion such as the person's work history, professional credentials, brokerage exam scores, and disciplinary records if applicable. It takes about five working days to receive this report.

If you can't uncover any problems, you like the firm and the broker, and they offer you the services you want at prices you feel are fair, it's probably time to open an account.

Opening a Brokerage Account

To open an account, you'll have to answer a lot of questions about your net worth, income, investment experience, age, and invest-ment objectives. Don't take offense at the personal nature of these questions. They're important. The broker is required to ask them due to New York Stock Exchange Rule 405, which says that stock-brokers must "know their clients" when recommending invest-ments. That's because an investment that's appropriate for one person may not be appropriate for another. For instance, a retiree with $10,000 to invest shouldn't invest in limited partnerships, but the forty-year-old with a $200,000 annual income just might. Be honest when answering the broker's questions; giving false information could only hurt you in the end.

When filling out the new account agreement, the broker will ask how much risk you want to assume and will give you cat-egories (such as growth, aggressive growth, or income) to choose from. Before choosing one, be sure you understand the implica-tions of each category. If you're retired and need income from your investments to pay your living expenses and you pick aggres-sive growth because you didn't understand the term, you'll end up with investments that are much too risky for your needs and you won't receive the amount of income you expect from your portfolio.

You'll also have to decide what type of account you're opening. If the account is yours only, you'll probably open an indi-vidual account. If you're opening it with a spouse, it may be joint tenants with right of survivorship. If the account belongs to you and your underage daughter, it could be a custodian account.

One other decision you have to make is whether you want the securities you purchase held in your name or in street name. If the account is in your own name, you may have to deal with receiving certificates when you buy stock. Street name, which means you won't receive certificates or be identifiable by the com-panies whose stock you own, is more convenient for most people.

Depending on the type of portfolio you plan to build, you may need to fill out additional forms. You'll probably want to open a sweep account, where dividends and interest payments can be deposited and where you can keep your cash until you need it to pay for securities. If you're planning to borrow funds from your broker to purchase securities, you'll need to fill out a form for a margin account, or if you want to give your broker discretion over your account to make trades without your approval (not a good idea at all), you'll be asked to fill out a discretionary account form.

After all the forms are completed, ask for copies. Be sure to get a copy of the new account form. You'll not be asked to sign this form, but it's important to review it to be sure all the information on it and the other forms is correct. If you told the stockbroker that your annual income is $50,000, is that what's listed? Is other information such as net worth, investment objectives, and age correct? If not, that incorrect information could create problems for you later.

If you've chosen to work with a full-service firm or even some discount firms, all the above steps apply and should be followed to help ensure you're hiring someone who's easy to work with and with whom you can build a long-term relationship. If you decided to use a deep discount firm, you won't have an individual broker to check out. That's even more reason to take time and care to check out the firm to be sure it's reputable.

If you're going to invest, you need to have a stockbroker. Using one who calls you over the phone with a great investment is not wise. Seek out a broker on your own terms, check him or her out through the NASD, and develop a long-term relationship. It won't guarantee a fraud-free investment future, but it'll certainly put the odds in your favor.

Mary L. Schapiro, President, National Association of Securities Dealers Regulation, Washington, D.C.

In 1996, NASD Regulation was created and charged with the responsibility of protecting investors by overseeing the activities of nearly all brokerage firms and stockbrokers in the country. We work to protect investors by regulating the securities industry in the following ways:

- *Regulation.* We have 1,650 employees who monitor and examine about six thousand member firms on a regular basis.
- *Enforcement.* The Department of Enforcement is our front-line investigative and prosecutorial group and houses a national team of attorneys and examiners. The department

formulates national enforcement policy and oversees the prosecution of disciplinary cases against brokers and their firms when wrongdoing is discovered.

- *Public disclosure program.* Investors are encouraged to check the disciplinary background of their brokers prior to doing business with them.
- *Rulemaking.* We develop rules that, once approved by the SEC, help ensure the integrity of member firms and the protection of investors. One of the rules pending with the SEC addresses the cold calling of investors by unregistered persons by seeking greater supervisory responsibility by firms and closely regulating what the callers may say to investors.
- *Investor education.* We have educational material available for investors on the NASD Regulation Web site: www.nasdr.com.

In 1997, we received fifty-five hundred customer complaints, and we investigated all of them. We permanently barred 428 individuals from the securities industry, and we suspended 236 individuals.

Although we do everything we can to ensure that our member firms and their employees are dealing honestly with the investing public, we can't do it alone. Investors should always check out a firm and stockbroker before doing business with them.

An investor who is wronged should first try to resolve the problem with the firm and then, if not fully satisfied, file a complaint with NASD Regulation to investigate further. Investors can check out stockbrokers and brokerage firms by calling 1-800-289-9999 or file a complaint using the NASDR Web site (www.nasdr.com) under the "Have a Complaint?" area.

A large percentage of our leads come from investors, and many of those complaints result in disciplinary action. We depend on investors to keep us informed. Only by working together will we be able to reduce fraud in the securities industry.

Checklist

While searching out and hiring a stockbroker to work with, have you:

☐ Determined your personal financial needs and investment objectives?

☐ Determined what type of brokerage firm you want to work with: full service, discount, or deep discount?

☐ Received information from two or three brokerage firms, read through the information, and then met with and asked pertinent questions of the stockbroker you believe best fits your needs?

☐ Called the NASD Public Disclosure Phone Center at 1-800-289-9999 to find out if the stockbroker or brokerage firm has had any disciplinary actions taken against them?

☐ Called the Better Business Bureau and your state's securities agency and asked if the stockbroker and the brokerage firm are both licensed or registered to sell securities in your state and if there have been any complaints filed against them?

☐ Been asked questions by the stockbroker as to your investment objectives, net worth, income, and other pertinent information when opening your brokerage account?

☐ Obtained copies of the new account form and other forms you signed when you opened your brokerage account, and checked them for accuracy?

If you answered yes to these questions, you've done a good job of finding and hiring a stockbroker who is probably honest, trustworthy, and willing to build a good working relationship with you for years to come.

CHAPTER 20

Finding and Working With a Trustworthy Financial Planner

What has not been examined impartially has not been well examined. Skepticism is therefore the first step toward truth.

DENIS DIDEROT, WRITER AND PHILOSOPHER

Many people believe that if they hire a financial planner, they won't have to worry about getting their own financial life in order. Instead, they can just hand it all over to someone else and forget about it. Here's what happened to one couple who did that.

Tom and Janet found someone who said he was a financial planner whom they thought they could trust. But instead of helping them invest their money in investments that were appropriate to their needs, he put 80 percent of their money into five limited partnerships that were much too risky for Tom and Janet's investment objectives. Not pleased with the planner's choice, they severed their relationship with him. They later learned that after they had ended the relationship, the planner telephoned a mutual fund company where they had their funds invested, impersonated

Tom, and obtained confidential information about them. Luckily, Tom and Janet were able to report the planner to the authorities before he could do any real damage.

Do You Need a Financial Adviser?

Just like with any other adviser you hire, you have to be careful. You took the time to find a reputable stockbroker you like and you're comfortable working with. If you decide to use a financial planner, you have to do the same work. But if you have a stockbroker, do you need a financial planner?

Stockbrokers are primarily skilled in the purchase and sale of securities. But your financial life is more than just stocks and bonds. It includes planning for other needs such as insurance, retirement, fringe benefits, and the eventual disposition of your estate. Many people handle all these aspects on their own. Others have an attorney, accountant, and insurance person, or others, each handling a piece of the whole. Others yet may hire someone who can look at the whole picture, create a master financial plan, and make sure each piece fits well with the other parts of the puzzle. That person is called a financial planner. A financial planner may also be a stockbroker, a life insurance agent, or a trust officer.

There are two services a financial planner can offer: financial planning advice and the implementation of that advice. If you hire the planner for advice only, he'll probably have you complete a detailed questionnaire. From that information he'll create a plan that fits your needs and turn it over to you. It's then your job to implement the plan by making the recommended investments, purchasing the recommended insurance, and having documents, such as wills or trusts, created. If you prefer, you can have the planner help you implement the plan and handle the details of putting everything in place.

Fraud in the Financial Planning Business

Just like any other professionals who deal with money, the great majority of financial planners are honest, trustworthy people. But there's always that small contingent of them who are not so honest. That can be frightening when you consider that this person will probably end up knowing more about the financial side of your life than you do. You definitely want someone who is honest, ethical, trustworthy, and competent.

One of the most prevalent types of fraud in the financial planning industry is the misrepresentation of credentials. The person may falsely claim to be a certified financial planner, a certified public accountant (CPA), or an attorney, or he may hide that he has had disciplinary actions taken against him. For instance, the authorities found one person who was still practicing as a financial planner after he had been fined $200,000 by the National Association of Securities Dealers (NASD), had pleaded guilty to one count of conspiracy to defraud, and had been issued two state orders requiring him to cease and desist from violations of the state securities act. Despite all that, he was still practicing.

Actually that's fairly easy to do because no regulatory agency has authority over financial planners as a whole. Therefore, the guy who delivers a pizza to your front door tonight can hang out a sign and advertise himself as a financial planner tomorrow. If he claimed to be an attorney, a stockbroker, or a CPA, he'd have to answer to the American Bar Association (ABA), the NASD, or the American Institute of Certified Public Accountants (AICPA). But as a financial planner, he's free to start doling out advice to anyone who will listen. Financial planners are regulated only by the services they provide. For instance, if a financial planner is a stockbroker, he'll be regulated by the NASD for that part of his job. If he sells insurance, he'll be regulated by the insurance industry. If he's a CPA, he'll be regulated by the AICPA. But no one agency has overall regulatory authority.

Some people have taken advantage of that lack of regulation because they see financial planning as a great way to steal other peoples' money. During the past couple of decades, the baby boomers have come of age; many are living in two-income families and pulling down huge salaries. A lot of the money has been spent, a little saved. As this generation begins to see that telltale gray appearing at their temples, they're beginning to realize they need to get their financial life in order. But they're busy working and raising their families, or they may not have expertise in areas such as investing, insurance, and estate planning. Their needs are fueling the growth of the financial planning industry.

And whenever a financial industry grows, there's always room for con artists.

Some con artists in the financial planning industry may have no expertise at all. Others may have expertise in only one area of financial planning and try to pawn that off to their customers. For instance, a group of insurance agents working out of Florida presented themselves as financial planners and began selling so-called retirement products in thirty-seven states. They targeted nurses and cosmetologists, and claimed to have a special retirement investment product that met the special needs of those groups. Their "special product" turned out to be insurance policies that weren't at all suited to retirement savings. In the end, the company agreed to refund as much as forty million to fifty million dollars in customers' premiums.

Financial planners who are con artists have been known to sell their clients abusive tax shelters, phony real estate partnerships, bogus money market accounts, nonexistent stocks and bonds, and complicated Ponzi schemes. One self-proclaimed financial adviser even had his own Saturday morning radio show, where he touted the great performance of a bogus mutual fund. His clients turned over four million dollars to him, a good portion of which he used to support his horse-racing business and gambling trips. Because of his high profile, he came to the attention of the authorities, was arrested, and was sentenced to eight years in prison.

How to Find a Financial Planner

A financial planner who is honest and competent can be a great asset. Most of us aren't sure if we're investing our money properly, if our wills are written so that our estates will pass on with minimal tax exposure, if the insurance we own is the correct type and amount for our situation, or if we'll be able to meet our financial goals and have enough money to finance our retirement. A good financial planner can answer all those questions and put our minds at ease. The key is to find one who is competent, honest, and ethical.

You can locate financial planners by asking for recommendations from friends or your professional contacts, such as your accountant or attorney. Or you can call an organization that can give you the names, addresses, and phone numbers of financial planners in your area. Four such organizations are:

Institute of Certified Financial Planners: 1-800-282-7526

International Association for Financial Planning: 1-800-945-4237

National Association of Personal Financial Advisors: 1-888-333-6659 (this organization deals specifically with fee-only financial planners)

American Institute of Certified Public Accountants, Personal Financial Planning Division: 1-888-777-7077

After you call one or all of these organizations and receive their lists, choose one or two planners you think you might like to work with and call them. Ask them to send you any brochures and information they have. Also ask for a copy of both parts of their Form ADV, which is the form they file with the SEC. It discloses their fees, investment philosophies, potential conflicts of interest, previous employment, and educational background. You can also obtain the planner's ADV form from the SEC:

Securities and Exchange Commission
Public Reference Branch
450 Fifth Street, N.W.
Washington, D.C. 20549
Fax: 1-202-628-9001
E-mail: publicinfo@sec.gov

Interviewing a Potential Planner

After you read through the materials the planner sends you, if you're still interested, call back and arrange a free consultation. Most will be willing to spend a half-hour with you to answer your questions. Following are some questions you might ask, which are based on material provided in a Certified Financial Planner Board of Standards brochure:

• *"What is your experience?"* Find out how long the person has been working as a financial planner, and what she was doing before. Try to find someone who has held the position for at least three years.

- *"What are your qualifications?"* Ask about formal educational background, professional training, and continuing education. Find out if the person has achieved any professional designations.

- *"Who are your clientele, and can you give me references?"* Be sure the planner's clients have somewhat the same needs you have to ensure he's familiar with your type of requirements. Always check references. Ask if the planner helped them meet their goals and about the quality of service they received. Don't be impressed by a planner who boasts a large number of clients. One bogus planner had twenty-five hundred clients whom he convinced to invest four thousand dollars each in an investment that turned out to be an abusive tax shelter scheme.

- *"What services do you offer?"* The services this person can offer will be determined by his licenses, credentials, and expertise. If retirement planning and estate planning are the areas in which you need assistance, find out if this person is qualified in those areas. Be careful of planners with extremely narrow expertise. One planner in Virginia claimed that his expertise was in repositioning assets for families seeking financial aid for their college-bound children. He used the $293,000 he collected from fourteen clients to pay for personal expenses, including a Mercedes.

- *"What is your approach to financial planning?"* Find out what types of clients this person typically works with, if she's aggressive or conservative in approach, and whether she plans to implement the plan she creates for you.

- *"Will you be the only person working with me?"* If there are assistants who will implement your financial plan, be sure to meet them. If the planner uses outside professionals, get their names and check them out. For example, if the planner does estate planning but is not an attorney, he'll have to send you to an attorney who can draw up a will, trust, or power of attorney.

- *"Have you ever been publicly disciplined for unlawful or unethical actions?"* Ask what organizations the planner is regulated by, and contact them to conduct a background check. For example, if the person is a stockbroker, you can call the

NASD public disclosure hot line (see Chapter 19) and check the person out.

- *"Can I have it in writing?"* Get a written statement that outlines what services the planner will provide.

- *"How will I pay for your services, and how much will it cost?"* How much you pay depends on your needs, but the planner should be able to give you a written estimate. There are basically three ways a financial planner can be compensated.

- A *fee-only* type of planner is compensated either by a flat rate to create and implement a plan or by the hour. Hourly rates range from less than one hundred dollars per hour to more than two hundred dollars per hour, depending, in part, on location. Typically planners in New York City charge more than planners in Kankakee, Illinois. If the planner charges a flat fee, it will probably add up to the same price as the hourly rate because it's based on the planner's hourly rate and the amount of time he believes it will take to complete the plan. The planner's fee for investing your money may also be based on a percentage of the assets he's controlling for you. That percentage could be as high as 3 percent. A fee-only planner does not represent insurance or brokerage firms and cannot sell you financial products; therefore, he's not biased in terms of selling you one product over another because of the commissions he would earn.

- A *commissions-only* type of planner is compensated through commissions charged to you when he sells you financial products. That means he is affiliated with a company such as a brokerage firm or insurance company and will sell you products through those affiliations. Some believe this is not a good arrangement because the planner may sell you financial products based not on your needs but on the level of commissions he earns.

- A *fee and commissions* type of planner is compensated by a combination of fees charged to create and implement a plan and commissions charged for selling you financial products.

Never agree to work with a financial planner who promises unrealistic returns, pressures you into quick decisions, is evasive in answering your questions, and makes recommendations without first studying your financial situation. Work only with a planner who will give you a plan that fits your individual needs rather than a computer-generated one-size-fits-all plan. Find someone who will give you choices in investments and will take the time to explain recommended investments to you. Seek out the financial planner you want to work with rather than giving your business to someone who calls you.

Checking Credentials

After you've met with the planner, if you still feel comfortable, you need to check credentials. The most well-known designation a financial planner can hold is that of Certified Financial Planner (CFP), bestowed by the Certified Financial Planner Board of Standards in Denver. To earn the CFP designation, a planner must pass a comprehensive exam, meet certain experiential requirements, agree to abide by a code of ethics, and complete continuing education requirements.

The Certified Financial Planner Board of Standards (1-888-237-6275) can tell you if a planner is indeed a CFP and if she's had any disciplinary actions taken against her. There are three disciplinary actions the board may take against a CFP:

- *Public censure or reprimand.* If the CFP has committed an infraction that is considered minor but viewed by the board to be in violation of its code, it can censure the person publicly by sending notification to newspapers and to any regulatory agency that may have authority over that person. It will also make the censure known in the CFP community nationwide by placing the person's name and the infraction on the board's Web site: www.cfp-board.org. Look under "CFP Board Report, Disciplinary Actions."
- *Suspension.* If the infraction is more serious, the person will receive a suspension, which she'll lose the right to use the CFP trademark for a period of time.
- *Revocation.* For extremely serious infractions, the person would receive a revocation, in which she'll lose the right to use the CFP mark forever.

Of course, it's important to remember that a financial planner has no obligation to achieve the CFP mark in the first place. It's not required to practice. Therefore, if a CFP has his designation revoked, he can still practice as a financial planner; he just can't call himself a certified financial planner.

There are two other highly reputable designations financial planners can achieve. One is the Chartered Financial Consultant (ChFC), which is bestowed by the insurance industry after a candidate passes a series of classes, takes continuing education courses, and agrees to abide by a professional code of ethics. The other is the Personal Financial Specialist (PFS), which is bestowed on CPAs by the AICPA.

If a planner tells you he's a Registered Investment Advisor (RIA), it means he's registered with the SEC. Don't put much stock in that credential. Registration under the Investment Advisor Act is required for any planner who charges a fee for giving financial planning advice. It simply means the person paid $150 to the SEC, filled out a form, and waited forty-five days for it to be processed. There are no tests or professional standards to be met to achieve registration. You can, however, ask for a copy of the person's Form ADV, which will give you helpful information.

To check credentials, you can also call the local Better Business Bureau and the state securities agency to find out if the person has a criminal history.

Beginning the Relationship

Once you've chosen a financial planner you want to work with, there are six steps the Certified Financial Planner Board of Standards recommends that you follow:

1. *Define your relationship.* Have the planner document in writing his responsibilities, your responsibilities, what services he will provide, how he will be paid, and how decisions will be made.
2. *Provide relevant information.* You need to give the planner information as to your financial situation, personal and financial goals, time frame for results, and level of risk tolerance. Be sure the long-term and short-term goals you offer are measurable.
3. *Evaluate your financial status.* The planner should analyze the information you've provided and create a plan that will steer you toward meeting your goals.
4. *Present recommendations.* Based on the information you provided, the planner should review his recommendations with you to ensure that you understand your options and can make

educated decisions. If a recommendation doesn't seem right or represents a major change from your current investments, reject it, or get a second opinion. A planner in Colorado, in conjunction with her husband, convinced eight of her clients to move $1.8 million from extremely safe certificates of deposit into nine extremely risky limited partnerships in residential mortgage loans. Those clients never recovered their money after she pleaded guilty to securities fraud and was sentenced to fifty-seven months in federal prison.

5. *Implement the plan.* The planner may implement the plan or guide you through the process of coordinating and implementing it. Be sure you understand all options presented and how a decision will affect other areas of your overall plan.

6. *Monitor results.* If the planner is in charge of monitoring the results of the plan, she should periodically report those results to you and adjust the process as required. The plan itself should also be reviewed periodically to ensure it's still on track.

Protecting Yourself From Dishonest Financial Planners

Your best bet is to choose a financial planner who is honest and trustworthy and won't cause you a problem. Obviously you can't do that with 100 percent certainty, but you can make your odds better by making certain choices and doing your homework. Although the CFP and other designations don't necessarily denote honesty, they do mean that this person took the time and effort to undertake additional education, passed a rigorous exam, met the work experience requirements, signed on to a code of ethics, and attends classes on a regular basis to keep current.

The typical con artist who wants to steal your money wants to do it quickly and with the least amount of effort. Many outright cons wouldn't take the time to achieve a professional designation. Therefore, if you start with a CFP, ChFC, or PFS, you may at least be looking at a better pool of financial planners.

If you believe you've been defrauded by a financial planner, report it immediately. If the person holds the CFP designation, report it to the Certified Financial Planner Board of Standards at 1-888-237-6275. They will investigate, and if they determine that a problem does exist, they can discipline the planner. If the planner holds other designations or has other credentials, such as being a CPA, an attorney, or an insurance agent, call the corresponding agencies and report the problem.

The key to finding a financial planner is taking your time and doing your homework. The time and effort you expend up front will be well worth the satisfaction you get by knowing you have a competent, honest person who can help you ensure your financial future is in order.

Alexandra Armstrong, Certified Financial Planner, Armstrong, Welch, and MacIntyre; Columnist for *Better Investing Magazine*, Author of *On Your Own: A Widow's Passage to Emotional and Financial Well-Being*

The reason I went into financial planning was that I didn't think you could make investment decisions without looking at someone's total financial picture. There are some financial planners who believe that if a client doesn't want a financial plan, that's fine, and the planner agrees to just manage the person's money. I don't agree with that.

I have people who come in and want me to manage their money, and I tell them I'm sorry, but I won't take anyone as a client unless that person has a financial plan created first. Without a plan, I can't do as good a job for the person. There's always a little grumbling because they don't want to do it. When they finally see the plan and realize how important it is, they agree.

Financial planning is a self-regulated industry. Since there is less-than-stringent regulation in the industry, it's important for consumers to be careful whom they work with. They should seek out someone who has at least bothered to obtain a reputable credential. That way they can check the person out with the agency that awarded that credential. Also, if they have a problem with the planner, they have the ability to make an appeal to that regulatory board. They should be sure to meet the financial planner they're considering in person. I am always amazed that people will do business with someone they've never met. They work so hard for their money; then they take the chance of working with a stranger and throwing it all away.

Checklist

When seeking out a financial planner to work with, have you:

❑   Determined whether you want a financial planner who offers only financial planning advice or one who also helps you implement that advice?

❑   Gotten recommendations of financial planners from advisers, friends, or organizations where financial planners register?

❑   Received and reviewed both parts of the Form ADV and other written information from two or three recommended financial planners regarding their services?

❑   Met with the financial planner and asked about the person's experience, qualifications, fee structure, and other pertinent issues?

❑   Asked for and called references?

❑   Checked out the financial planner with the NASD Public Disclosure Hotline at 1-800-289-9999, the CFP Board of Standards at 1-888-237-6275, or other professional organizations based on the financial planner's credentials?

❑   Checked with the Better Business Bureau and the state securities agency to determine if the financial planner has a criminal history?

❑   Been asked by the financial planner to complete a detailed questionnaire before beginning the financial planning process?

If you answered yes to these questions, you've probably found a financial planner with whom you can establish a productive relationship in building your financial future.

CHAPTER 21

Looking to the Future

Of all hard things to bear and grin,
The hardest is being taken in.

PHOEBE CARY, AMERICAN POET

Fast-forward to the year 2020. You're surfing the Internet and find an investment offer that looks interesting. It's a start-up company that's raising money to manufacture a new type of golf club. The club's designers guarantee the club will reduce a golfer's handicap by one third. The secret of the club is twofold. First, it's made out of a combination of alloys that gives the club the perfect strength and flexibility required to allow the action of the swing to propel the ball farther. Second, the design of the club is such that it improves accuracy in the placement of the ball by 30 percent.

These new clubs have been tested by several professional golfers, all of whom have endorsed them. The company already has $11.5 million in orders from country club professional shops and well-known golf equipment retailers around the world. A comprehensive advertising plan is in place, just waiting for the manufacturing process to begin. The company has acquired a manufacturing plant in Bolivia, where labor costs are low, but it needs to raise a few million dollars to convert the plant and get it up and running.

Because of the superiority of the clubs, the prominent endorsements the company has acquired, and the major advertising campaign that's ready to roll, the company projects that the sale of the clubs will generate enough income to give investors a 40 percent return the first year and probably higher in later years.

The investment sounds good to you, but you decide to check it out before you commit. You pick up the phone and call your attorney. After pressing buttons to get you through fourteen separate menus, the receptionist's face pops up on your phone vision screen as she answers your call. She smiles and tells you Mr. Jones is out of town and won't be back until next week. You don't bother to leave a message. If only you hadn't fired your stockbroker a few years ago, you could get his advice. Of course, you've really saved a lot of money by getting rid of him and doing all your trades on-line.

You turn back to the Internet and notice that the golf club investment offer has an investment deadline of the day after tomorrow. You begin to rationalize. Golf has become extremely popular and is now the fastest-growing leisure activity in the country. Every golfer you know would happily pay big bucks to reduce his handicap by a third.

You've really been concerned lately that your retirement nest egg may not be sufficient for you to retire in a few years as you planned. A 40 percent return would certainly give it a good boost. Besides, you know a good investment when you see one. Why should you miss out on a great investment opportunity just because your attorney is out of town? You quickly invest fifty thousand dollars.

Six months later when you realize you've been scammed, you call your state securities agency and find that it is already aware of the scam. The truth is that there's no super golf club, no professional golfers were ever involved, and the company doesn't exist. The authorities do know that the people who perpetrated the scam were out of Italy, but no one knows who they are. Even if they did know who they are, however, your state agency has no jurisdiction in Italy. So you call the SEC, but the person you talk to tells you the same thing: the SEC's jurisdiction ends at the U.S. borders. Besides, the authorities, both state and federal, have enough resources to investigate only a small percentage of the scams perpetrated each year. Therefore, they concentrate on those scams that affect the most people. A scam that stole four million dollars from five hundred investors is insignificant in terms of the devastation some con artists wreak on thousands of investors for millions and millions of dollars. Yes, you've lost your life savings, but no one can help you now.

That's not a very rosy picture, but it's one that may come to pass in the not-too-distant future. In the next ten, fifteen, or twenty years, the enforcement agencies will have to deal with four growing problems: the growth of the Internet, the internationalization of fraud, the growth of the pool of potential victims, and the elimination of the investors' safety net.

Growing Problems

Growth of the Internet

Cyberinvesting is booming. According to Forrester Research of Cambridge, Massachusetts, at the end of 1998 there were more than eighty on-line brokerage firms holding 5.3 million accounts worth approximately $233 billion. That was up from eighteen on-line firms with 1.5 million accounts with $111 billion in assets in 1996. The big draw is that the average commission charge for trading on-line is just seventeen dollars per trade.

As investors turn to the Internet for their investment needs, the con artists are right beside them. But because the Internet creates a borderless, global trading environment, it's nearly impossible for law enforcement and regulatory agencies to identify con artists and prosecute them. A con artist on the Internet can claim to be anyone, anywhere, and no one can prove differently. As cyberinvesting increases, so will the fraud, but regulators will have insurmountable problems in trying to identify con artists, gather evidence, establish jurisdiction and venue, and attribute responsibility. Problems that now exist with unlicensed broker and agent activity, market manipulation, insider trading, and other types of fraud perpetrated over the Internet will explode. Having the ability to reach millions of people at once with fraudulent offers will be very appealing to the con artists as they become more computer savvy and figure out new ways to separate you from your money by working on-line.

Internationalization of Fraud

Con artists are already starting to cross borders to protect themselves while they victimize people in the United States. That creates jurisdictional problems for authorities. Stopping a fraud that's conducted from another country means coordinating different laws and different systems, attributing responsibility, and even determining international definitions for specific terms such as *offer, sale,* or *disclosure.* Currently, on the regulatory side, there is no consistency in the accounting systems used, in disclosure, or in the regulatory structure.

The growth of the Internet and the internationalization of fraud go hand in hand in creating an almost impenetrable haven for con artists. Bill McDonald, enforcement director for the California Department of Corporations, the state securities regulator for California, says his nightmare is going into a situation with a search warrant and finding a room full of computers, but all the books and records are hidden in a network in Amsterdam, and all the transactions have been run through an offshore bank in Belize.

Growth in the Pool of Potential Victims

On the other side of the spectrum is the growing audience of potential victims. Employees of past generations worked for the same company for a lifetime, retired, and lived off their pensions and Social Security checks. But today the average person changes jobs seven times in his lifetime and doesn't necessarily have a retirement nest egg built up. The future of Social Security is also questionable. The direction of our society is that more people will have to take responsibility for their own financial futures and retirements and will have to handle their own investments.

Unfortunately, the American education system isn't teaching financial survival skills. As more people try to invest without having the skills required to understand what is a good investment and what is a fraud, the con artists will have their choice of victims. And they will begin mass-marketing those frauds rather than focusing on delivering their scams on an individual basis.

Elimination of the Investor's Safety Net

As electronic trading continues to become more popular, there will be fewer reasons for an investor to have a one-on-one relationship with a broker. That creates risk for the investor. A stockbroker is a middleman who provides the integrity of a licensed entity that's regulated and required to keep books and records, that can be held responsible, and that has a real existence. If there's a problem, the investor has somewhere to go to get recourse. With the impersonalization of electronic trading, the individual will lose his voice and his ability for recourse.

In the future, individuals will have more responsibility, less protection, and probably less security in their old age. Con artists already target senior citizens. As the baby boomers age and realize they may not have enough money to maintain their current lifestyles, they may try to go for the huge return. Years of sustained prosperity have lulled many baby boomers into a false sense of security. They believe the market will work magic for them and help them build their fortunes.

There may already be an inordinate amount of sales practice abuses in the brokerage industry, such as lack of suitability and lack of risk disclosure, that are being masked by a bull market. A bear market may bring a day of reckoning and could have a serious, long-term impact.

On the Positive Side . . .

Not all types of fraud will expand, however. Telemarketing fraud, one of the most popular types of fraud today, may even diminish. One-on-one frauds will give way to mass-marketing of frauds. But that's not the only problem fraudulent telemarketers may face. Part of the reason fraudulent telemarketers are successful is that they hide behind their anonymity. A nineteen-year-old in a T-shirt and jeans working out of a boiler room can read from a script and pawn himself off as a senior vice president who's sitting in the penthouse office of a luxurious office building on Wall Street. If technology brings vision screen phones into our homes so that we can see each other face-to-face during phone conversations, the telemarketer's scam will become more difficult. Having the ability to look them in the eye, see their appearance and their surroundings, and use visual cues will give the investor an advantage.

Potential victims, while probably more plentiful in the future, may be more difficult to convince. Baby boomers seem to be more skeptical than their parents and aren't as willing to trust others. They also aren't as concerned about being impolite and are more willing to hang up on a con artist. That healthy dose of skepticism may save them money.

On the regulatory side, changes need to be made. Legislation, treaties, or information-sharing agreements among countries need to be put in place. Jurisdictional issues will need to be addressed. While John Wayne used to have to stop at the Mexican border when he was chasing the bad guys, that problem, while not quite as blatant, does still exist. Con artists still have access to secret bank accounts, tax shelter havens, and countries where criminals can't be extradited for financial crimes. Countries will have to share information and remove the impediments that prohibit successful prosecution of fraud.

White-collar criminals are being prosecuted now more than ever before. Sentences of five, ten, or fifteen years are becoming prevalent. But the possibility of a prison term doesn't seem to be a deterrent to con artists, because they don't think they'll ever get caught. If they don't get caught, why should they care if the prison sentence for their crime is one year or fifty years? And they may be right. Regulators have the resources to investigate and prosecute only a few scams, so many con artists go free. In fact, the elderly woman who is accosted on the street and has her purse containing fifty dollars stolen has a much better chance of getting help from law enforcement officials than if she had her life savings stolen by a con artist.

We all have to take steps to protect ourselves from fraud. Resources for checking out an investment, a firm, and a salesperson are abundant. By doing just a little, you can protect yourself so much. Education is the key. Educate yourself, and educate your children. If our children grow up with the knowledge and expertise they need to be able to identify a fraud and avoid it, the pool of future victims for con artists to target will dwindle.

There's no reason not to invest, but do it with care by exerting a little time and effort and by seeking out professionals who can help guide you in building your financial future.

In this book you've read about people who have learned tough lessons. We can all learn from their experiences. Whether you're making investments, starting a franchise, taking out a loan, or hiring a stockbroker or financial planner, approaching it in an intelligent and studied way can do more to protect you than one hundred investigators, one hundred prosecutors, and one thousand prison cells can.

No one cares more about your financial future than you do. Therefore, it's your responsibility to take charge and cover your assets. I wish you luck in building your financial future. May you always stay fraud free.

Marc Beauchamp, Communications Director, North American Securities Administrators Association, Washington, D.C.

This country needs to be much more aggressive about investor education. In our schools we teach drivers ed, sex ed, and phys ed. Why not investor ed? Children need to understand that you don't get rich quick, but that you get rich slowly by working hard, being very skeptical about the investments you make, and taking responsibility for your own financial future.

As a start, in a coordinated effort with the National Association of Securities Dealers and the nonprofit Investor Protection Trust, we've developed a program called Financial Literacy 2001, a model curriculum for high school seniors aimed at teaching them the fundamentals of personal finance. We're just rolling it out into hundreds of schools, but plan to have it ultimately taught in thousands of schools.

However, each state has different curriculum standards, so our challenge is to convince them that children need to be armed with this type of knowledge before venturing out on their own. While Financial Literacy 2001 is aimed at high school seniors, teaching money management is something you could start as early as first or second grade. Children love money, and teaching them how to make it, save it, invest it, and protect it will help them for the rest of their lives. We need to reduce the number of potential victims. Through education, we can do that, generation by generation.

Checklist

In the future, will you:

❑ Check out any investment offer, loan offer, business offer, or other opportunities that are proposed to you before making a commitment?

❑ Be careful in accepting offers that come to you over the Internet?

❑ Be wary of offers you receive when you can't verify the location of the salesperson or the company?

❑ Restrain yourself from trying to hit the big one or going for the big return?

❑ Utilize the abundance of resources available to you for checking out an investment, a company, and a salesperson?

❑ Educate yourself and your children so you have the knowledge and expertise needed to identify a fraud and avoid it?

If you answered yes to all of these questions, you have high odds of remaining fraud free.

GLOSSARY

*It's better to lose an investment opportunity than to
lose your money.*

GARY BERTRAND, AUTHOR'S HUSBAND

advance fee fraud Fraud in which a con artist charges a victim,
either an individual or small business, an advance fee to obtain a
loan and then never funds the loan.

affinity fraud Fraud targeted toward a group of people who have
a close relationship, a connection, or a common origin.

arbitration A system for resolving disputes in which the two parties submit their disagreement to an impartial panel for binding resolution.

asset misappropriation Employee fraud in which the employee
steals or misuses the company's assets for his own benefit.

ATM con Scam in which the con artist obtains the victim's personal identification number through devious means, then with-
draws money from that person's account. Also, a scam in which the
victim is sold an ATM under the false impression that it can be
leased or operated for a profit.

bank examiner scam Scam in which someone posing as a bank examiner asks the victim to withdraw money from the bank in an effort to help the examiner expose a dishonest employee.

boiler rooms Inexpensive office space where con artists set up banks of phones to use for telemarketing scams.

bribery Employee fraud in which an employee, with the help of an outside accomplice, steals money from the employer through kickbacks or bid-rigging schemes.

bucket shops Scam in which the con artist takes an investment order over the phone, instructs the victim to send in a check, hangs up, and throws the order away.

build-out scam Investment scam in which the con artist claims to have a license from the Federal Communications Commission and is raising money to build transmission towers, lay cable, garner customers, or whatever activities are required to get the business up and running.

business opportunity fraud Fraud in which the con artist promises to supply the victim with the equipment, supplies, and customers needed to start a business.

Certified Financial Planner (CFP) A financial planner who has achieved the CFP designation by passing an exam, agreeing to abide by a code of ethics, and completing thirty hours of continuing education every two years.

charity fraud Fraud in which the con artist claims to represent a charity, but the charity doesn't really exist or a very minimal portion of donations are used for the charity's cause.

chartered financial consultant (ChFC) A person who has achieved the ChFC credential, which is bestowed by the insurance industry after the candidate passes a series of classes, takes continuing education courses, and agrees to abide by a professional code of ethics.

churning The illegal practice followed by some stockbrokers of buying and selling stocks for no purpose other than to generate commissions.

clearing firms Large brokerage houses that handle administrative paperwork, such as processing trades and providing customers with confirmations, account statements, and other documentation, for other brokerage firms.

commissions only A method of compensation in which a financial planner is compensated only by commissions charged when he sells the client financial products.

commodity fraud Scams that involve the sale of commodities through either options or futures contracts.

con artist A person who swindles, scams, and steals from others.

conflict-of-interest schemes Fraud in which a high-level corporate executive steals money from the company through a vendor in which he has an ownership position.

corruption Employee fraud that requires the assistance of an outside accomplice.

cramming Scam in which bogus charges show up on a person's phone bill for services the person never agreed to purchase, such as voice mail, paging, personal 800 numbers, or even non-phone-related services, such as charges for club memberships that bill through the phone company.

credit card fraud Fraud in which the con artist writes an increased amount on a credit card receipt or steals the victim's credit card number and then makes purchases on that card.

deep discount stockbroker A brokerage firm that offers no services other than to fill buy and sell transactions for a very low commission.

discount stockbroker A brokerage firm that offers clients fewer services than a full-service firm in exchange for lower commissions.

economic extortion schemes A fraud in which someone requires a bribe as a condition of doing business.

fee and commissions Method of compensation in which a financial planner is compensated through a combination of fees charged to create and implement a plan and commissions charged for selling the client financial products.

fee only Method of compensation in which a financial planner is compensated either by a flat rate or by the hour to create and implement a financial plan for a client.

Financial Literacy 2001 A model curriculum for high school seniors aimed at teaching them the fundamentals of personal finance.

financial planner A person who creates and/or implements a personalized financial plan for clients, including strategies for investing, reducing taxes, purchasing insurance, and doing estate planning.

Forex market The Foreign Exchange Market, which trades foreign currencies. No regulatory agency monitors this market.

Form ADV The form that financial planners file with the Securities and Exchange Commission that discloses information about their fees, investment philosophy, potential conflicts of interest, previous employment, and educational background.

franchise A company that, for a fee, offers individuals assistance in starting their own business by supplying them with a recognizable trade name, site location assistance, standard operating procedures, training, advertising, and a supplier of inventory.

franchisee A person who purchases a franchise.

franchisor A person who sells franchises.

fraudulent disbursements Employee fraud in which the employee steals money from the employer by creating fraudulent expense accounts or a dummy company to which he writes checks.

fraudulent statements Fraud in which a high-level executive alters the company's books to make the company's performance appear better than it really is.

full-service stockbroker A brokerage firm that offers services such as research reports, investment ideas, and portfolio monitoring for a higher level of commissions.

futures contract An agreement to receive or deliver a certain amount of a commodity at a specific price at some date in the future.

hedgers Producers and end users of commodities who enter into futures contracts as a form of insurance to control income and expenses, but also with the intent of taking delivery of the commodity.

high-tech fraud Investment scams that focus on new and complicated technology-related products.

identity theft The stealing of someone's personal information such as Social Security number, date of birth, bank account numbers, or mother's maiden name and using that information to create havoc with the person's credit rating, reputation, and life.

illegal gratuity schemes Fraud in which an employee accepts a reward for giving a vendor part of the company's business.

Internet fraud Fraud perpetrated over the Internet in an effort to reach multiple numbers of victims at the same time.

IPRCs International Postal Reply Coupons, issued by postal services for customers who are sending mail from one country to another. IPRCs were the backdrop of the first Ponzi scheme.

larceny A crime in which an employee steals from the employer without any real attempt to cover up the crime.

lottery scam A scam in which the con artist claims to be able to obtain licenses from the Federal Communications Commission for new products through a lottery or auction.

magazine subscription fraud Scam in which the victim unknowingly purchases multiple subscriptions to magazines at outrageously high prices.

mediation An informal process in which a single mediator assists two parties in determining a mutually agreeable resolution to a dispute. The mediator does not make a final decision and cannot impose a settlement on the parties.

micro-cap stock fraud Fraud that involves the sale of very small company stocks that are very risky, typically generate no revenues, and have no short-term prospects of generating any revenues.

Nigerian or **419 scam** Scam in which the con artist claims to be an official of a foreign government who is offering to transfer millions of dollars from an overpaid government contract into the victim's bank account in order to get the money out of the country.

offshore bank investments Scam in which the con artist promises the victim extremely high returns to invest money in financial instruments through banks outside the United States.

option A contract that gives an investor the right, but not the obligation, to buy or sell a specified quantity of a commodity at a specific price within a specified period of time.

payment packing Scam in which a car dealer sells the victim additional services or products when buying a car and hides those extra costs in the monthly financing payments.

pay-per-call services Scam in which the victim is enticed into calling a 900 number and is then charged an exorbitantly high amount for the call.

personal financial specialist (PFS) Credential bestowed by the American Institute of Certified Public Accountants on certified public accountants who meet certain qualifications.

Ponzi scheme An investment scam in which the promoter pays off the earliest investors with the money he collects from later investors.

postal fraud Scam in which the con artist scans newspaper obituaries and then sends newly widowed victims bills or packages that he claims the deceased spouse had ordered.

promoter Person or firm that induces investors to purchase securities or other investments.

public censure or **reprimand** Punishment given to a certified financial planner who has committed a minor infraction that is in violation of the Certified Financial Planner Board of Standards code. Notification is sent to newspapers and regulatory agencies.

pump and dump Scam in which a con artist pumps up the price of a stock by touting it and selling it to others, and then dumps the stock when the price increases.

pyramid scheme A passive investment scheme in which investors are sold the ability to become salespeople who earn commissions for each new salesperson they recruit.

registered investment advisor (RIA) Credential that means the person registered with the Securities and Exchange Commission by paying $150, filling out a form, and waiting forty-five days for it to be processed. There are no tests or professional standards to be met to achieve registration.

reload or **recovery room scam** A scam in which a con artist claims that for a fee, he can help a victim recover money lost in a previous fraud.

revocation Punishment doled out by the Certified Financial Planner Board of Standards to certified financial planners who commit extremely serious infractions. In a revocation, the planner loses the right to use the CFP trademark forever.

Rule 405 An ethical concept set forth by the New York Stock Exchange stating that all brokers must "know their clients" because an investment that is suitable for one client may not be appropriate for another.

self-liquidating loan A loan in which a portion of the principal of a loan is used to purchase a zero coupon bond. When the bond matures, the money is used to pay off the loan. Self-liquidating loans don't work and don't exist.

selling away Scam in which a stockbroker sells clients investment products that don't go through the brokerage house he's licensed with.

skimming Employee fraud in which the employee makes a sale and converts the money to his own use before the sale ever gets recorded in the company's books.

slamming Scam in which victims are tricked into changing their phone service to another carrier without even realizing they've done it.

Social Security fraud Scam in which the con artist charges the victim a fee for services that are free through the Social Security Administration.

speculators Investors who trade futures contracts purely as speculative investments with no intention of ever taking possession of the commodities behind the contracts.

storage scam A scam in which the investor buys a commodity from a con artist who supposedly takes possession of the goods and stores them. In reality, the con artist takes the investor's money but never purchases the commodity.

sucker or **mooch list** List of people who have been victims of fraud. Con artists sell these lists to each other, with some names costing as much as twenty-five dollars.

suspension Punishment doled out by the Certified Financial Planner Board of Standards to a certified financial planner who has committed a fairly serious infraction. In a suspension, the person loses the right to use the CFP trademark for a specified period of time.

telemarketing fraud Fraud perpetrated over the telephone.

theft Scam in which a stockbroker sells stock out of a client's account and pockets the proceeds.

$12.95 brick Scam in which a con artist poses as a deliveryperson with a neighbor's C.O.D. package. The victim pays the C.O.D. charge, only to learn that the package is not for a neighbor and that it contains a worthless brick.

unauthorized trades Scam in which a stockbroker buys or sells a security without the permission of the client.

unsuitability Scam in which the stockbroker sells a client investments that are not suitable in meeting the investment objectives the client has outlined.

Agencies and Organizations

American Association of Retired Persons
601 E Street, N.W.
Washington, D.C. 20049
1-800-424-3410
Web site: www.aarp.org

American Bar Association
750 North Lake Shore Drive
Chicago, Illinois 60611
1-312-988-5000
Web site: www.abanet.org

American Institute of Certified Public Accountants
Personal Financial Planning Division
Harborside Financial Center
201 Plaza Three
Jersey City, New Jersey 07311
1-888-777-7077
Web site: www.aicpa.org

American Institute of Philanthropy
4905 Dell Ray Avenue, Suite 300
Bethesda, Maryland 20814
1-301-913-5200
Web site: www.charitywatch.org

American Society of CLU & ChFC
270 South Bryn Mawr Avenue
Bryn Mawr, Pennsylvania 19010
1-800-392-6900
Web site: www.financialpro.org

American Society of Travel Agents (ASTA)
Consumer Affairs Department
1101 King Street, Suite 200
Alexandria, Virginia 22314
1-703-739-8739
Web site: www.astanet.com

Certified Financial Planner Board of Standards
1700 Broadway, Suite 2100
Denver, Colorado 80290
1-888-237-6275
Web site: cfp-board.org

Children's Partnership
1351 Third Street Promenade, Suite 206
Santa Monica, California 90401-1321
1-310-260-1220
Web site: www.childrenspartnership.org.

Commodity Futures Trading Commission
3 Lafayette Centre
1155 21st Street, N.W.
Washington, D.C. 20581
1-202-418-5000
Web site: www.cftc.gov

Council of Better Business Bureaus
4200 Wilson Boulevard
Arlington, Virginia 22203
1-703-276-0100
Web site: www.bbb.org

Direct Marketing Association
Telephone Preference Service
P.O. Box 9014
Farmingdale, NY 11735-9014
1-202-955-5030

Direct Marketing Association
Mail Preference Service
P.O. Box 9008
Farmingdale, NY 11735-9008
1-202-955-5030

Equifax
P.O. Box 105873
Atlanta, Georgia 30348
1-800-685-1111

Experian
P.O. Box 2104
Allen, Texas 75013-2104
1-800-682-7654

Federal Bureau of Investigation (FBI)
The phone number of your local office is listed on the first page of
the phone book.
Web site: www.fbi.gov

Federal Communications Commission
Common Carrier Bureau
Consumer Complaints
Mail Stop Code
1600 A2
Washington, D.C. 20554
1-888-225-5322
Web site: www.fcc.gov

Federal Trade Commission
Sixth Street and Pennsylvania Avenue, N.W.
Washington, D.C. 20580
1-202-326-3650
Web site: www.ftc.gov

Institute of Certified Financial Planners
3801 East Florida Avenue, Suite 708
Denver, Colorado 80210
1-800-282-7526
Web site: www.icfp.org

International Association for Financial Planning
5775 Glenridge Drive N.E., Suite B-300
Atlanta, Georgia 30328
1-800-945-4237
Web site: www.iafp.org

International Franchise Association
1350 New York Avenue
Washington, D.C. 20005
1-800-543-1038
Web site: www.franchise.org

National Association of Insurance Commissioners
120 West 12th Street, Suite 1100
Kansas City, Missouri 64105
1-816-842-3600
Web site: www.naic.org

National Association of Personal Financial Advisors
355 West Dundee Road, Suite 200
Buffalo Grove, Illinois 60089
1-888-333-6659
Web site: www.napfa.org
E-mail: info@napfa.org
This organization deals specifically with fee-only financial planners.

National Association of Securities Dealers (NASD)
1735 K Street, N.W.
Washington, D.C. 20006
Public Disclosure Phone Center
1-800-289-9999
Web site: www.nasd.com

National Association of Securities Dealers (NASD)
Dispute Resolution Offices:
125 Broad Street, 36th Floor, New York, New York 10004,
1-212-858-4400
10 South LaSalle Street, 20th Floor, Chicago, Illinois 60603,
1-312-899-4440
515 East Las Olas Boulevard, Suite 1100, Fort Lauderdale, Florida
33301,
1-954-522-7403
525 Market Street, Suite 300, San Francisco, California 94105,
1-415-882-1234
300 South Grand Avenue, Suite 1620, Los Angeles, California
90071,
1-213-613-2680
1735 K Street, N.W., Washington, D.C. 20006, 202-728-8958

National Charities Information Bureau
19 Union Square West
New York, New York 10003
1-212-929-6300
Web site: www.give.org
E-mail address: ncib@bway.net

National Consumers League
1701 K Street, N.W., Suite 1200
Washington, D.C. 20006
1-202-835-3323
Web site: www.natlconsumersleague.org

National Foundation for Consumer Credit
8611 Second Avenue, Suite 100
Silver Spring, Maryland 20910
1-888-269-6251
Web site: www.nfcc.org

National Fraud Information Center (NFIC)
P.O. Box 65868
Washington, DC 20035
1-800-876-7060
Web site: www.fraud.org

National Futures Association (NFA)
200 West Madison Street
Chicago, Illinois 60606
1-800-621-3570 (within Illinois, 1-800-572-9400)
Disciplinary Information Access Line (DIAL):
1-800-676-4NFA between 8:00 A.M. and 5:00 P.M. (central time).
Web site: http://www.nfa.futures.org

National White Collar Crime Center
1001 Boulders Parkway, Suite 450
Richmond, Virginia 23255
1-800-221-4424

North American Securities Administrators Association
1 Massachusetts Avenue, N.W., Suite 310
Washington, D.C. 20001
1-202-737-0900
Web site: www.nasaa.org

Opt Out Request Line
1-888-567-8688

Privacy Rights Clearinghouse
1717 Kettner Avenue, Suite 105
San Diego, California 92101
1-619-298-3396
Web site: www.privacyrights.org

Public Investors Arbitration Bar Association
1111 Wylie Road, #18
Norman, Oklahoma 73069
1-888-621-7484
Web site: www.piaba.org

Securities and Exchange Commission
450 Fifth Street
Washington, D.C. 20549
1-800-732-0330
Web site: www.sec.gov

Securities Arbitration Group, Inc.
National Mediators Group
330 Washington Boulevard
Marina Del Rey, California 90292
1-800-222-4724

Social Security Administration
Office of the Inspector General
6401 Security Boulevard, Room 300
Altmeyer Building
Baltimore, Maryland 20260-2100.
Automated line: 1-800-772-1213

Trans Union Corp.
Merchants Association Credit Bureau
P.O. Box 3307
Tampa, Florida 33601
1-813-273-7700

U.S. Postal Service
Chief Postal Inspector
475 L'Enfant Plaza, S.W.
Washington, D.C. 20260
1-202-268-4267

White Collar Crime 101
1-800-440-2261

INDEX